SBAC

SMARTER BALANCED

GRADE 7 ELA

By Dr. Frances Lin, Ph.D.

About the Author

Frances Lin is a middle school educator who is an ambassador of writing for young authors. She is a poet, critical theorist, and novelist who also enjoys writing for the educational world. She lives in Central California with her muses—Kayla, Achilles, and Comet. This is her first professional book, and she is currently working on her poetry books and young adult novel.

Acknowledgments

The author would like to acknowledge the love and support of her family and friends. Without them, this book would not have happened. Special thanks to her mother, Young Sil Lin, for encouraging her throughout the process. This book is dedicated to her most precious muse—Tess, who showered her with love and with inspiration as she typed away each day.

The Smarter Balanced screenshots, on pages 4, 5, 6, 7, and 9, as well as the Smarter Balanced Performance Task Scoring Rubrics on pages 173–182, are reprinted with permission courtesy of The Regents of the University of California. The publishing of this information does not represent an endorsement of products offered or solicited by Barron's Educational Series, Inc.

ISBN: 978-1-4380-1034-2
Library of Congress Control Number: 2017942580

Date of Manufacture: August 2017
Manufactured by: B11R11

Printed in the United States of America
9 8 7 6 5 4 3 2 1

Contents

Introduction

Understanding the SBAC Test:
Information that Every Student Should Know

This testing guide is geared toward students and parents who are interested in learning about the Smarter Balanced Assessment that is typically administered by their teachers at the end of the school year in the spring months. Thus, seventh grade students would expect to be tested around April depending on the testing schedules in their state. This testing guide can be used by students in order to prepare for the SBAC test. SBAC represents the following words—Smarter Balanced Assessment Consortium. This is the overarching label given to the tests created at the national level. States may refer to the SBAC test with other identifiers specific to that area. For example, in California, the SBAC test is part of the California Assessment of Student Progress and Performance (CAASPP) system. Many educators in this state call the test the CAASPP test. However, the SBAC test is the actual test, and it is based on the Common Core standards that are used nationwide. The CAASPP is simply a system used to house the SBAC for administration along with resources for students, parents, and teachers to use in California.

The SBAC test is very different from previous standardized tests that have been administered in the past. The general idea behind the SBAC test is to assess how well students can use critical thinking skills and 21st century knowledge and tools to demonstrate college and career readiness. This means that students will have to show how they can problem-solve and think creatively in order to respond to assessment items successfully whether they be selected-response or constructed-response. Students must be capable of using computer knowledge and tools to answer technology-enhanced items, and all of these skills must be used to illustrate the abilities of a student who is college and career ready. These are very different ideas from the assessments administered in the past. Once you are familiar with the setup, standards, items, and format of the SBAC test, you will find it easier to take the test at the end of your seventh grade year.

The SBAC test is aligned with the English Language Arts (ELA) Common Core standards for designated grade levels. You will find a copy of the ELA standards in Appendix A. The ELA Common Core standards are grouped for grades 6-12. However, there is a column specifically designated for seventh grade students. All of the practice test items in this testing guide are based on the Common Core standards, so you will be practicing with items that you may encounter on the actual SBAC test. For example, a Common Core standard is that a student can determine a theme of a text and analyze the development of that theme throughout the narrative. This testing guide may then provide a passage for you to read, and the items, or questions, that follow will ask you to use your knowledge in order to demonstrate your understanding and knowledge of this standard. All items in this testing guide will reflect the content and skills of the Common Core standards because this will be the case in the actual SBAC test that you will take in the spring of your seventh grade year.

There are four claims that the SBAC test is based on, and it is important to note and to understand these claims as they are the umbrella over the SBAC test. In ELA, the four claims are grouped in the following areas: 1) reading analytically; 2) writing effectively; 3) speaking and listening purposefully; and 4) conducting research. These are the four areas that are the focus of the SBAC test. In other words, these are the areas that the SBAC purposefully looks for when assessing your knowledge and skills obtained during your seventh grade school year. It is important that you understand what these claims are asking of you, so that you can be prepared when the actual assessment comes around.

The first claim is stating that students can engage in close reading using analytical skills to understand complex literary and informational text passages. Lexile ranges, or text complexity levels, vary depending on the portion of the test being administered. Students are expected to be able to comprehend these texts by using critical thinking skills in order to dig deeper into the text than expected in past assessments. Students will need to interpret and to infer deeper meanings of these passages in order to respond successfully to each item. This means that students will need to form educated responses that reflect underlying meanings not directly stated in the texts. Using the tools in this testing guide can help students achieve this.

The second claim deals with writing responses that are effective and adequately supported by textual evidence for different writing purposes and audiences. This means that the student's written responses need to be strong in organization and purpose. The student must appropriately address the audience who will be reading the writing pieces, and ample textual evidence should be provided in order to support all claims and assertions. The assessment will have a wide range of writing tasks for each student to complete that are based on many passages and texts. Remember that effective writing is expected in this particular claim. You will find writing tasks spread throughout the different assessment sections. Some will be short, and others may be more extensive with longer writing tasks. You will find multiple tools in this testing guide to help you in crafting effective writing responses on this assessment.

The third claim focuses on a student's ability to use speaking and listening skills effectively for various purposes and audiences. In this claim, College and Career Readiness (CCR) anchor standards expect that students know how to prepare for collaborative conversations with others with clear and persuasive expression of ideas. Students will be expected to evaluate information that is represented by various media and formats and to examine a speaker's viewpoints and logic. Finally, students must be able to present information that is supported by textual or visual evidence and that is organized and well developed. The purpose and audience will need to be appropriately addressed. Different media and visuals of information will also be a focus of this claim.

The fourth and final claim is the research and inquiry assessment where students are to investigate information and to analyze information that can be later presented effectively and appropriately based on the task. Students must demonstrate mastery in posing research questions and in presenting a logical sequence of claims and assertions that are supported by the texts and multimedia information provided. Students should be able to dig deeper into inquiry and to think critically about the multiple forms of research that are included in the item content. Students will oftentimes need to connect all four of these claims together in order to create effective and successful responses to all of the sections of the test. This is just an overview of the general information that you will need to know in order to understand what the SBAC test is asking of you.

Major Components of the SBAC ELA Test

There are four major item types on the SBAC test. Entire items are simply the collective presentation of questions, stimulus, answers, scoring criteria, and sources. The stimulus is the text passage, source, and or visual provided to give the student the context of the item. The four major item types are selected-response items, constructed-response items, technology-enhanced items, and performance tasks. There is a separate chapter for each item type except for the technology-enhanced items in this testing guide. More details on these item types follow this chapter, but a brief overview will be helpful in framing what the SBAC test will look like.

Selected-response items are similar to multiple-choice questions. There will be a question or prompt, and answer options will be listed underneath the item. The stimulus is the passage, text, or graphic that provides the context for the test questions or items; for example, the reading passage before a set of questions is the stimulus. Students will read the stimuli for context and then will select the response that best answers the question. Constructed-response items also have stimuli, but there will typically be a text box for students to type in responses. Thus, students are constructing or making a response in their own words with the exception of textual evidence pulled from the stimuli. The following screenshots show examples of selected-response and constructed-response items.

Figure 1.1 also provides an example of a constructed-response item where the student must create dialogue that does not already exist. The student is expected to craft a dialogue exchange between characters in order to demonstrate the ability to use critical thinking skills and creativity to come up with a possible conversation that could happen between two characters.

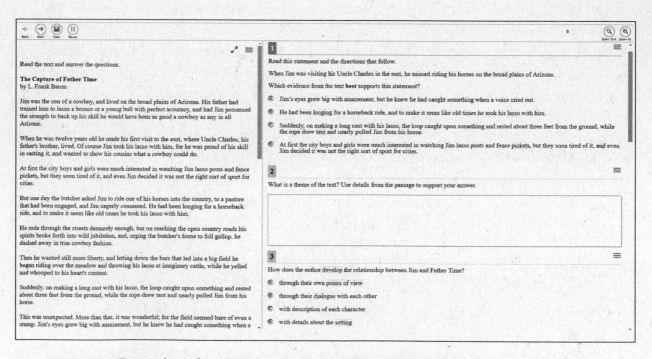

Figure 1.1—Examples of selected-response and constructed-response items.

---

17 ≡

A student is writing a narrative for a literary magazine about two friends on a hot day. Read the draft of the introduction and complete the task that follows.

A Hot Day

Joe lounged outside under a tree, the only area having a significant amount of shade. It was only 9:00 a.m., but the temperature had already passed the 80-degree mark and was rising rapidly. Weather forecasters on the news programs had predicted that the heat wave would continue through the next couple of days. They had even provided safety precautions to take during times of high temperatures. Listeners had been advised to exercise only in the early morning hours and in the late evening hours. They had also been instructed to drink a large quantity of water to stay hydrated. Joe was still debating what activity he wanted to do when his friend George arrived.

Write the dialogue that might have occurred when George walked up to Joe.

Figure 1.2–An example of a constructed-response item asking the student to write dialogue between two characters based on the stimulus.

Technology-enhanced items are questions or prompts that ask the student to click or to drag information from one spot to another. They are interactive and require that the student is comfortable with using the computer. The following screenshot shows a technology-enhanced item where a student is asked to click on precise words.

---

18 ≡

A student is writing an article about baboon troops for a student science magazine. Read the paragraphs from the draft of the article and complete the task that follows.

Baboons are a large type of monkey. They stay/reside in groups called "troops" which are composed of dozens of baboons. Troops usually sleep, travel, feed, and socialize together.

Baboons spend their days cleaning one another and hunting for food. In the morning, adult baboons sit in small groups picking and eating/nibbling bits of dirt, leaves, dry skin, and salt off one another's hair and skin while the young baboons play. Then, the troop moves together catching lizards, butterflies and grasshoppers to eat. In the hottest part of the day, the baboons choose a cool place to linger and rest before continuing their search for food. The baboons groom/fix one another again before retiring in the evening.

For **each** underlined pair of words, click on the word that is the **most** precise.

Figure 1.3–An example of a technology-enhanced item that requires the student to select a precise word and click on it.

Performance tasks are the final item that a student will encounter on the SBAC test. Performance tasks oftentimes require that a classroom activity is completed prior to the test. The student can expect to read quite a few reading passages with a range of multimedia stimuli. Although the next screenshot is not from a performance task, it does illustrate how various media can be used to provide context to the question or even a performance task. In this example, a student is directed to listen to a presentation before answering questions.

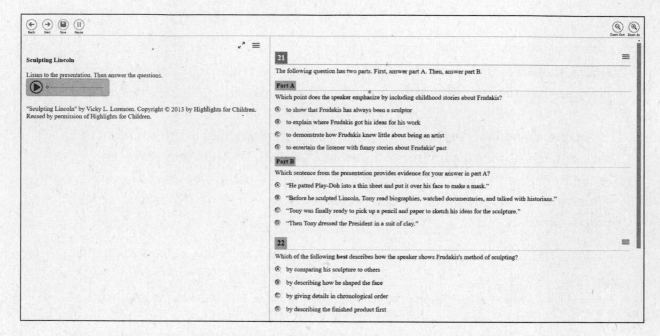

Figure 1.4—This example shows how a student must listen to a presentation before answering selected-response and technology-enhanced questions.

The final screenshot provided also gives you an idea of what could potentially be added to a performance task. In this example, the item asks for students to evaluate sources in a research inquiry context. The performance task usually comprises multiple stimuli and tasks.

---

27   ≡

A student is writing a research report about ozone levels in the atmosphere. Read the paragraph from her report and the directions that follow.

Ozone is a type of oxygen that rests in Earth's upper atmosphere. This protective layer of oxygen serves a very important purpose for climate control. The ozone in the atmosphere works to block ultraviolet rays from the Sun and lessens their effects on crops, animals, and people. Ultraviolet rays have a shorter wavelength than regular light and can be harmful if people are over-exposed to them. The ozone layer is constantly shifting, which creates small holes at both the North and South Poles of Earth. As such, some of the coldest places on Earth are bombarded with ultraviolet rays from the Sun and have little protection from them.

Which source would **most likely** give the student more information for her report?

Ⓐ   www.oxygenuses.com

  While oxygen is found in our atmosphere, it has numerous uses in the medical, industrial, chemical, automotive, and environmental lines of work.

Ⓑ   www.ozonelayer.com

  Explore how the ozone layer must be protected in order to safeguard our planet from the dangers of ultraviolet rays.

Ⓒ   www.saveourpoles.com

  Join with us in our appeal to ban substances that harm the ozone layer which can lead to irreversible damage to animal life at the North and South Poles.

Ⓓ   www.avoidtherays.com

  Learn how to protect yourself from the Sun's harmful ultraviolet rays in every season, no matter your climate.

Figure 1.5–This example gives the student a glimpse of what possibly can be asked in a performance task based on research and inquiry.

How to Use this Book Effectively

Using this testing guide effectively will help you prepare for the SBAC test successfully. Each chapter covers the important features of the various item types that the SBAC uses to measure student learning. Each chapter also gives you some strategies to use while taking the test. For example, you will learn about the "pie" method for constructed-response items. The few minutes it takes to complete a "pie" chart could significantly change the quality of your responses. The testing strategies are also meant for you to use while you practice in this testing guide.

There is also a section in chapter five that is meant to give you specific writing exercises that could dramatically change how well you write on the test or in general. These writing tasks, prompts, and strategies will increase your confidence level in dealing with constructed-response items, with performance task writing, and with writing in general. It is recommended that you actively engage in the activities in this testing guide to maximize your personal test-taking development. Remember that taking tests requires skills, and honing these skills through practice and familiarization will help you immensely as you move forward to the summative SBAC test in the spring of your seventh grade year. Walk through all of the activities in this testing guide, and you will see that there are strategies and tips that can support you in taking tests in general as well as the SBAC.

Preparing to Take the Test

The best preparation in taking the test is taking a deep breath and trusting that the learning you did all year in your seventh grade ELA class will help you through this process. After noting this, think about all of the information that you will have learned about the test once you complete reading and engaging in the activities in this testing guide. You will be more than prepared. You will have familiarized yourself with the way the SBAC is formatted, with the major components of the SBAC test, and with the testing strategies that will lead you to success. Remember that you learned these skills already. Now it is a matter of demonstrating that you did indeed master these skills through your responses.

Once you have completed the reading and writing activities in this testing guide, you should be very confident in taking the SBAC test. The philosophy of the SBAC test is different from past assessments, but it is definitely doable. All students can be successful in taking this test as long as they are aware of how and what it is asking of them. Read on, and good luck on your journey!

Selected-Response Tasks (Multiple-Choice)

Understanding the Selected-Response Section

The selected-response section is the equivalent to what is formerly known as multiple-choice. Selected-response items will have a question, answer options, and a stimulus. Before delving into testing strategies, it may help to look at the anatomy of a selected-response item. Remember that items include different parts. We will look at them right now. First, look at the following screenshot of a selected-response item in its entirety. We will take it apart in the next step.

---

16 ≡

A student is writing an argumentative essay for English class about the need for punctuality. Read the draft of the essay and complete the task that follows.

Why to Show Up On Time

There are many reasons why our school should stress punctuality. Since learning how to manage time is critical to our futures, having students arrive on time to class would have many benefits. If punctuality were encouraged, this school would be a better place.

Having a tardy rule is basic to enforcing punctuality, and our school does have a tardiness policy. It is not so much what our schools are doing, but what they are not doing that's working. Do students really understand why being 10 or so minutes late to class is harmful to *them* as individuals? By being ready when class begins, students will be able to focus their time on learning.

Revise the student's draft about the need for punctuality. Choose the sentence that gives the **best** evidence to improve support of the student's claim.

Ⓐ Tardiness is defined as not being in the appropriate classroom seat when the school bell rings.

Ⓑ There are many schools in the area that have a tardy rule, including East Warren and Smithfield Middle Schools.

Ⓒ According to the US Department of Education, students who are in class on time have a better chance of earning good grades than students who are tardy.

Ⓓ There is really no need for rewarding punctuality among the masses because students already know that they must arrive to their classes promptly as a school requirement.

Figure 2.1—An example of a selected-response item.

Figure 2.1 displays what you will see on the SBAC test when looking at a selected-response item. The stimulus in this example is the student argumentative essay that is provided. Remember that a stimulus is the text or passage that gives context to the question. The task is embedded in this item, and it specifically asks for you to select the answer choice that best reflects evidence that would support the student claims. The selections that are incorrect are the distracters, and the options are the possible answers. Finally, the stem of the task is the statement of the prompt that asks you to revise the student draft and to select the best evidence to support the student's assertions.

Notice how the SBAC test gives you a task for a selected-response item that differs from past assessments. The item asks for you to think critically about what would serve as the best revision for this essay. Now that you understand the basic anatomy of a selected-response item, it is time to look at testing strategies that will help you in selecting the correct options as often as possible.

Testing Strategies that Work

1. Read the question, task, or prompt first before you even read the stimulus, or passage. This will pinpoint what you need to be able to demonstrate in the selected-response item. In the example on page 9 (Figure 2.1), you would determine that you are looking to revise the essay by finding evidence that would best support the student claims. If you know this before you even read the student essay, then you know what you are looking for in the stimulus. Also, if you are reading a passage that is paired with questions, you will know in advance what to look for as you take the time to read the stimulus, or reading passage. This is an important way to start the selected-response test process.

2. While you are reading the question or prompt, really think about what the question is asking you to do. Is it asking you to analyze, evaluate, or examine? Look at the action verbs, and try to decide what the gist of the question is asking you to do. If you understand what the task is asking you to do, then you have an idea of what the focus of the question is. It is always good to concentrate on the purpose of the question. Once you know the purpose, you will have a better idea of what to look for in the answer options. Remember that the SBAC test is different from tests of the past. There is a wide range of prompts and tasks that go beyond simple reading comprehension questions.

3. After reading the stimulus, or passage, revisit the question in the item. Try to think about a possible answer to the question without looking at the actual answer options. This will give you an idea about what you think would be a good answer to look for before rereading the options. It is always a good idea to do this before answering the question. Once you have an idea, compare it to the answer options provided on the SBAC test.

4. Now that you have an idea of what the answer could potentially be and now that you have determined the purpose of the question, you can look at the answer options to see what you think would work the best. Be mindful of distracters. In our look at the anatomy of a selected-response item, we noticed that the distracters are the incorrect options in a question, task, or prompt. As you probably already know, eliminating the distracters that are most obvious to you is a first step. This means that you should cross out the answers that you know are not correct. This is part of the old process of elimination strategy. It is best to narrow down your choices as much as possible. This will increase the likelihood of you selecting the correct answer.

5. Once you select an answer option for the selected-response item, reread the question, prompt, or task. Does your selected option answer the question? Does it demonstrate a skill that the question has asked you to show? These are important questions to ask yourself as you reevaluate the answer that you selected. After answering a selected-response item, always reread the question and answer to ensure that you have indeed selected the correct answer option.

Computer-Adaptive Testing Effects

As you have seen in previous screenshots, the selected-response items could be mixed in with constructed-response items, which we will look at more closely in the next chapter. However, this testing guide is designed to give you practice on one type of question at a time, so that you can focus on the testing strategies specific to that item type. Remember that there may also be technology-enhanced items and tasks as well that are interspersed throughout the SBAC test. This may require that you click on precise words or complete a chart. These are all part of the test as well.

Finally, this is a computer-adaptive test. This means that the items will get increasingly more challenging as you correctly answer questions and respond to tasks and prompts, or the items will get easier as you respond incorrectly to the questions or prompts. It would be best for you not to worry about how easy or how hard the questions are. Just work through the SBAC test the best you can, and do not waste time trying to figure out if the items are getting harder or easier.

SELECTED-RESPONSE TESTING PRACTICE

In this section, you will be given multiple opportunities to practice your testing strategies on selected-response items. Follow the guidelines that you read about in the previous sections as you respond to the questions, prompts, or tasks in each item. There will be a short explanation of why the correct answer is the right choice. There are no scoring criteria for the selected-response items, so a brief explanation will be included per question.

Passage 1—Narrative Passage

Directions: Read the following narrative passage. Use the testing strategies that were included in the previous section to practice answering the selected-response items that follow the reading passage. Look for the rationale after you respond to each question, prompt, or task.

The Jungle Book
by Rudyard Kipling

Now Rann the Kite brings home the night

   That Mang the Bat sets free—

The herds are shut in byre and hut

   For loosed till dawn are we.

This is the hour of pride and power,

   Talon and tush and claw.

Oh, hear the call!—Good hunting all

   That keep the Jungle Law!

Night-Song in the Jungle

   It was seven o'clock of a very warm evening in the Seeonee hills when Father Wolf woke up from his day's rest, scratched himself, yawned, and spread out his paws one after the other to get rid of the sleepy feeling in their tips. Mother Wolf lay with her big gray nose dropped across her four tumbling, squealing cubs, and the moon shone into the mouth of the cave where they all lived. "Augrh!" said Father Wolf. "It is time to hunt again." He was going to spring down hill when a little shadow with a bushy tail crossed the threshold and whined: "Good luck go with you, O Chief of the Wolves.

And good luck and strong white teeth go with noble children that they may never forget the hungry in this world."

It was the jackal–Tabaqui, the Dish-licker–and the wolves of India despise Tabaqui because he runs about making mischief, and telling tales, and eating rags and pieces of leather from the village rubbish-heaps. But they are afraid of him too, because Tabaqui, more than anyone else in the jungle, is apt to go mad, and then he forgets that he was ever afraid of anyone, and runs through the forest biting everything in his way. Even the tiger runs and hides when little Tabaqui goes mad, for madness is the most disgraceful thing that can overtake a wild creature. We call it hydrophobia, but they call it dewanee–the madness–and run.

"Enter, then, and look," said Father Wolf stiffly, "but there is no food here."

"For a wolf, no," said Tabaqui, "but for so mean a person as myself a dry bone is a good feast. Who are we, the Gidur-log [the jackal people], to pick and choose?" He scuttled to the back of the cave, where he found the bone of a buck with some meat on it, and sat cracking the end merrily.

"All thanks for this good meal," he said, licking his lips. "How beautiful are the noble children! How large are their eyes! And so young too! Indeed, indeed, I might have remembered that the children of kings are men from the beginning."

Now, Tabaqui knew as well as anyone else that there is nothing so unlucky as to compliment children to their faces. It pleased him to see Mother and Father Wolf look uncomfortable.

Tabaqui sat still, rejoicing in the mischief that he had made, and then he said spitefully:

"Shere Khan, the Big One, has shifted his hunting grounds. He will hunt among these hills for the next moon, so he has told me."

Shere Khan was the tiger who lived near the Waingunga River, twenty miles away.

"He has no right!" Father Wolf began angrily–"By the Law of the Jungle he has no right to change his quarters without due warning. He will frighten every head of game within ten miles, and I–I have to kill for two, these days."

"His mother did not call him Lungri [the Lame One] for nothing," said Mother Wolf quietly. "He has been lame in one foot from his birth. That is why he has only killed cattle. Now the villagers of the Waingunga are angry with him, and he has come here to make our villagers angry. They will scour the jungle for him when he is far away, and we and our children must run when the grass is set alight. Indeed, we are very grateful to Shere Khan!"

"Shall I tell him of your gratitude?" said Tabaqui.

"Out!" snapped Father Wolf. "Out and hunt with thy master. Thou hast done harm enough for one night."

"I go," said Tabaqui quietly. "Ye can hear Shere Khan below in the thickets. I might have saved myself the message."

Father Wolf listened, and below in the valley that ran down to a little river he heard the dry, angry, snarly, singsong whine of a tiger who has caught nothing and does not care if all the jungle knows it.

Selected-Response Items

Read each question carefully. Review the answer options, and go through the testing strategies provided in this chapter. Practice using them as you go through the process of selecting the correct answer(s).

1. How does the setting of this story shape the characters and the plot? Select **two** responses that show how the setting shapes the characters and the plot.

   ☐ A. The setting introduces the main characters and describes the personalities of the characters.
   ☐ B. The setting explains how Tabaqui is a mad, wild creature.
   ☐ C. Tabaqui enjoys angering other characters while making mischief throughout the hills.
   ☐ D. The setting shows how the wolves and the tigers are fighting for the hunting grounds in the area.
   ☐ E. The fighting illustrates the struggle between different characters.
   ☐ F. The setting frames the background of the story.
   ☐ G. The setting advances the plot with a conflict in the "Law of the Jungle."

2. How does the author develop and contrast the points of view in the characters? Select **two** responses that demonstrate the development and contrast of the points of view of two characters.

☐ A. Father Wolf is a strong and powerful character, whereas Tabaqui is an inconsequential character that has little power.

☐ B. Mother Wolf is contrasted with Father Wolf to show the balance between two characters who need to work together in order to rule the land.

☐ C. The author describes Tabaqui, the jackal, with details that tell the reader what he is likely to think as he is characterized as unpredictable.

☐ D. The cubs are important characters because the power of Father Wolf will be passed on to them.

☐ E. Father Wolf has an opposing point of view to Tabaqui, and the author contrasts these points of view.

☐ F. Tabaqui recognizes the cubs, which is important to the plot of the story.

3. Why is it important for the author to describe Tabaqui's joy in mischief made in the wolf cave where he "spitefully" makes a statement to anger the wolves?

○ A. Tabaqui is a major character, and the author characterizes him in a way that will add interest to the story. Characterization is an important part of a narrative.

○ B. The author has developed this character throughout the passage, and he portrays this character with consistency as Tabaqui makes the comment about Shere Khan to upset Father Wolf, which sets up the theme.

○ C. Father Wolf is a powerful character in the story, and Tabaqui angers him, which illustrates the character of the jackal with more emphasis and moves the story forward.

○ D. It is important for the author to show Tabaqui's character because he is unpredictable and adds character to the story with his different personality as compared to the other characters.

4. Read the following sentence. Highlight **three** examples of context clues that provide hints about the meaning of the word "despise."

   It was the jackal–Tabaqui, the Dish-licker–and the wolves of India despise Tabaqui because he runs about making mischief, and telling tales, and eating rags and pieces of leather from the village rubbish-heaps.

5. Read the following sentence from the text.

   He scuttled to the back of the cave, where he found the bone of a buck with some meat on it, and sat cracking the end merrily.

   Which words are synonyms for the root word, "scuttle"? Select **all** that apply.

   ☐ A. run
   ☐ B. jump
   ☐ C. fall
   ☐ D. scurry
   ☐ E. saunter
   ☐ F. meander

6. Read the following text from the passage.

   "All thanks for this good meal," he said, licking his lips. "How beautiful are the noble children! How large are their eyes! And so young too! Indeed, indeed, I might have remembered that the children of kings are men from the beginning."

   Now, Tabaqui knew as well as anyone else that there is nothing so unlucky as to compliment children to their faces. It pleased him to see Mother and Father Wolf look uncomfortable.

   Highlight the **two** sentences that support how Tabaqui enjoys causing mischief.

7. Read the following sentence from the passage.

   "They will scour the jungle for him when he is far away, and we and our children must run when the grass is set alight. Indeed, we are very grateful to Shere Khan!"

   What does the word "scour" mean?

   ○ A. rub fiercely
   ○ B. search fervently
   ○ C. rush hurriedly
   ○ D. clean enthusiastically

   (Answers are on pages 147–148.)

Passage 2—Nonfiction Passage

Directions: Read the following nonfiction passage below. Use the testing strategies that were included in the previous section to practice answering the selected-response items that follow the reading passage. Look for the rationale after you respond to each question, prompt, or task.

Remarks
by Bill Nye

Looking over my own school days, there are so many things that I would rather not tell, that it will take very little time and space for me to use in telling what I am willing that the carping public should know about my early history.

I began my educational career in a log school house. Finding that other great men had done that way, I began early to look around me for a log school house where I could begin in a small way to soak my system full of hard words and information.

For a time I learned very rapidly. Learning came to me with very little effort at first. I would read my lesson over once or twice and then take my place in the class. It never bothered me to recite my lesson and so I stood at the head of the class. I could stick my big toe through a knot-hole in the floor and work out the most difficult problem. This became at last a habit with me. With my knot-hole I was safe, without it I would hesitate.

A large red-headed boy, with feet like a summer squash and eyes like those of a dead codfish, was my rival. He soon discovered that I was very dependent on that knot-hole, and so one night he stole into the school house and plugged up the knot-hole, so that I could not work my toe into it and thus refresh my memory.

Then the large red-headed boy, who had not formed the knot-hole habit went to the head of the class and remained there.

After I grew larger, my parents sent me to a military school. That is where I got the fine military learning and stately carriage that I still wear.

My room was on the second floor, and it was very difficult for me to leave it at night, because the turnkey locked us up at 9 o'clock every evening. Still, I used to get out once in a while and wander around in the starlight. I did not know yet why I did it, but I presume it was a kind of somnambulism. I would go to bed thinking so intently of my lessons that I would get up and wander away, sometimes for miles, in the solemn night.

One night I awoke and found myself in a watermelon patch. I was never so ashamed in my life. It is a very serious thing to be awakened so rudely out of a sound sleep, by a bull dog, to find yourself in the watermelon vineyard of a man with whom you are not acquainted. I was not on terms of social intimacy with this man or his dog. They did not belong to our set. We had never been thrown together before.

After that I was called the great somnambulist and men who had water-melon conservatories shunned me. But it cured me of my somnambulism. I have never tried to somnambule any more since that time.

There are other little incidents of my schooldays that come trooping up in my memory at this moment, but they were not startling in their nature. Mine is but the history of one who struggled on year after year, trying to do better, but most always failing to connect. The boys of Boston would do well to study carefully my record and then–do differently.

Selected-Response Items

Read each question carefully. Review the answer options, and go through the testing strategies provided in this chapter. Practice using them as you go through the process of selecting the correct answer(s).

8. Which of the following responses **best** depicts the central ideas in the text? Select **three** responses that apply.

☐ A. Growing up is a hard journey, but it has its rewards.

☐ B. Developing as a student into a man is a complex process that requires thought and hard work.

☐ C. The author finds himself in a place that he enjoys because of his experiences.

☐ D. School can be a challenging situation.

☐ E. Reflection is a part of this process as the author contemplates how his younger years shaped his life.

☐ F. It is the obstacles that make people who they are.

☐ G. Younger days are definitely something to share as they show how some men come to be successful.

9. Which details **best** demonstrate the development of the central ideas over the course of the passage? Select **four** responses that apply.

- ☐ A. The author provides details about his class rivals to illustrate how school from his younger days taught him how to endure.
- ☐ B. Military school provided structure and discipline to the author.
- ☐ C. His idea of somnambulism, or sleepwalking, adds charm to the author's account of his reflective and contemplative nature as a young man.
- ☐ D. He reminisces about the knot-hole to show how school was very challenging.
- ☐ E. The watermelon patch was a wake-up call for the author as he realized that he was on property not meant for a somnambulist.
- ☐ F. He was embarrassed to be in the watermelon vineyard.
- ☐ G. The log house details show how the author tries to develop.

10. What role does figurative language play in this passage?

- ○ A. The author uses symbolism of the knot-hole to illustrate how the author is weak and cannot overcome his obstacles.
- ○ B. The author uses descriptive language to portray his younger days and the challenges that went with them.
- ○ C. The author uses similes to characterize his early school rival in a way that adds interest and a colorful description that would otherwise be less effective.
- ○ D. The author uses figurative language throughout the passage to describe how he overcame his childhood fears.

11. Read the following sentence from the text.

Finding that other great men had done that way, I began early to look around me for a log school house where I could begin in a small way to soak my system full of hard words and information.

What type of language is used here? Select **three** responses that apply.

- ☐ A. figurative language
- ☐ B. hyperbole
- ☐ C. imagery
- ☐ D. simile
- ☐ E. metaphor
- ☐ F. symbolism

12. Read the following sentence from the passage.

This became at last a habit with me. With my knot-hole I was safe, without it I would hesitate.

Which of the following words **best** describes the meaning of the word, "hesitate," as it is used?

○ A. pause
○ B. cease
○ C. feel uncertain
○ D. sigh

13. Read the following sentence from the passage.

A large red-headed boy, with feet like a summer squash and eyes like those of a dead codfish, was my rival.

Circle the **two** similes that are provided in this sentence.

14. Read the following sentences. Which sentences support the author's message that developing as a person can be a challenge? Select **two** that apply.

☐ A. Learning came to me with very little effort at first.
☐ B. It never bothered me to recite my lesson and so I stood at the head of the class.
☐ C. Then the large red-headed boy, who had not formed the knot-hole habit went to the head of the class and remained there.
☐ D. My room was on the second floor, and it was very difficult for me to leave it at night, because the turnkey locked us up at 9 o'clock every evening.
☐ E. I was never so ashamed in my life.
☐ F. Mine is but the history of one who struggled on year after year, trying to do better, but most always failing to connect.

(Answers are on pages 148–149.)

On Your Own

Selected-Response Items

Now it is your turn to demonstrate what you have learned from this chapter and in your seventh grade class. Read each question carefully. Review the answer options, and go through the testing strategies provided in this chapter. Practice using them as you go through the process of selecting the correct answer.

Passage 3—Nonfiction Passage

1873 Speech on Women's Rights
by Susan B. Anthony

Friends and fellow citizens: I stand before you tonight under the indictment for the alleged crime of having voted at the last presidential election, without having a lawful right to vote. It shall be my work this evening to prove to you that in thus voting, I not only committed no crime, but, instead, simply exercised my citizen's rights, guaranteed to me and all United States citizens by the National Constitution, beyond the power of any state to deny.

The preamble of the Federal Constitution says:

"We, the people of the United States, in order to form a more perfect union, establish justice, insure domestic tranquility, provide for the common defense, promote the general welfare, and secure the blessings of liberty to ourselves and our posterity, do ordain and establish this Constitution for the United States of America."

It was we, the people; not we, the white male citizens; nor yet we, the male citizens; but we, the whole people, who formed the Union. And we formed it, not to give the blessings of liberty, but to secure them; not to the half of ourselves and the half of our posterity, but to the whole people— women as well as men. And it is a downright mockery to talk to women of their enjoyment of the blessings of liberty while they are denied the use of the only means of securing them provided by this democratic-republican government—the ballot.

For any state to make sex a qualification that must ever result in the disfranchisement of one entire half of the people, is to pass a bill of attainder, or, an ex post facto law and is therefore a violation of the supreme law of the land. By it the blessings of liberty are forever withheld from women and their female posterity.

To them this government is not a democracy. It is not a republic. It is an odious aristocracy; a hateful oligarchy of sex; the most hateful aristocracy ever established on the face of the globe; an oligarchy of wealth, where the rich govern the poor. An oligarchy of learning, where the educated govern the ignorant, or even an oligarchy of race, where the Saxon rules the African, might be endured; but this oligarchy of sex, which makes father, brother, husband, sons, the oligarchs over the mother and sisters, the wife and daughters, of every household—which ordains all men sovereigns, all women subjects, carries dissension, discord, and rebellion into every home of the nation.

Webster, Worcester, and Bouvier all define a citizen to be a person in the United States, entitled to vote and hold office.

The only question left to be settled now is: Are women persons? And I hardly believe any of our opponents will have the hardihood to say they are not. Being persons, then, women are citizens; and no state has a right to make any law, or to enforce any old law, that shall abridge their privileges or immunities. Hence, every discrimination against women in the constitutions and laws of several states is today null and void, precisely as is every one against Negroes.

Selected-Response Items

Read each question carefully. Review the answer options, and go through the testing strategies provided in this chapter. Practice using them as you go through the process of selecting the correct answer(s).

15. Which of the following statements **best** captures the central ideas that are presented in this speech?

   O A.   The author depicts the lives of women who have been unjustly treated although it is legal for them to be excluded from voting.

   O B.   The author expresses how women are a valid group in the country that has not been permitted to exercise a right that is supported by the U.S. Constitution—voting.

   O C.   The author exclaims how challenging the world has been for many groups other than white, male citizens in the country.

   O D.   The author admonishes the injustice of voting rights with an angry recollection of past problems in the nation.

16. What kind of writing technique does the author use when she speaks of the democracy which is really "an odious aristocracy; a hateful oligarchy of sex?" Select **all** responses that apply.

- ☐ A. The author uses similes to compare a democracy to an oligarchy.
- ☐ B. The author uses imagery to demonstrate how the world can get better.
- ☐ C. The author is using comparative language to enhance an effect of strong persuasion from exaggeration.
- ☐ D. The author uses symbolism to explain how unfair the world has been in the past.
- ☐ E. The author is using repetition to communicate a point that supports the central idea of her speech.
- ☐ F. Injustices are depicted as abolished through imagery.

17. What does the author mean when she uses the word "hardihood?" What is the effect that she creates in her speech by using this language? Select **two** responses that **best** apply.

- ☐ A. The author uses this word to emphasize how important it is to allow different groups to vote in the country.
- ☐ B. The author uses this language to communicate how only a bold and daring human would disagree that women are persons.
- ☐ C. The author embeds this word within the argument that women are persons, which makes the opponents seem unreasonable.
- ☐ D. The author uses symbolism to represent the injustices that have occurred in this nation.
- ☐ E. The language causes an effective sensory feeling of these injustices.
- ☐ F. The language introduces onomatopoeia where hardihood sounds like the bold and daring opponents who disagree with the author.

18. Josephine is writing an essay about the central ideas in Susan B. Anthony's speech. The following paragraph is from her introduction. Read the paragraph, and complete the tasks that follow.

Susan B. Anthony delivered an emotional and effective speech to depict the injustice of not permitting women to vote in the country. She describes her hope for a world that recognizes women as citizens. She exaggerates and repeats certain words and phrases to make an effective argument.

Part A

What would be an effective thesis statement for Josephine's introduction?

- ○ A. In her speech, Susan B. Anthony expresses the need for justice and equality for all of humanity.
- ○ B. Susan B. Anthony explains how the current situation is poor and depraved.
- ○ C. This speech demonstrates the use of a lot of figurative language.
- ○ D. Susan B. Anthony describes the negative consequences of others in the world.

Part B

Which of the following sentences would **best** support Josephine's thesis statement? Select **all** that apply.

- ☐ A. The preamble of the Federal Constitution says: "We, the people of the United States, in order to form a more perfect union, establish justice...."
- ☐ B. And we formed it, not to give the blessings of liberty, but to secure them; not to the half of ourselves and the half of our posterity, but to the whole people—women as well as men.
- ☐ C. It was we, the people; not we, the white male citizens; nor yet we, the male citizens; but we, the whole people, who formed the Union.
- ☐ D. And it is a downright mockery to talk to women of their enjoyment of the blessings of liberty while they are denied the use of the only means of securing them provided by this democratic-republican government—the ballot.
- ☐ E. Friends and fellow citizens: I stand before you tonight under indictment for the alleged crime of having voted at the last presidential election, without having a lawful right to vote.

19. Read the following sentence from the text.

By it the blessings of liberty are forever withheld from women and their female posterity.

What **best** defines the word "posterity"? Select **all** that apply.

☐ A. female strengths
☐ B. the disfranchised
☐ C. future generations of people
☐ D. injustice
☐ E. victims
☐ F. future women

(Answers are on pages 149–150.)

Constructed-Response Tasks

Understanding the Constructed-Response Section

The constructed-response section of the SBAC test will be based on the Common Core principles that appear in the other test sections. The constructed-response section will include reading passages followed by questions that will test your ability to use the information found in the passage to create a well-written, successful response. This is part of the computer-adaptive testing that was introduced in the multiple-choice section of this testing guide.

Remember, the SBAC test is measuring how well you are able to think critically and to analyze the passages by judging how well-written, clear, and meaningful your written response is. Many times, this section of the test is expecting a response that is well-constructed and informative. Depth of Knowledge, one of the Common Core principles, will be assessed in the constructed-response section of the test. This means that it is important for you to use more complex thinking skills such as analysis and critical interpretation. This chapter will prepare you to respond to these types of questions successfully.

Another Common Core principle that is very important in the constructed-response testing section is evidence-based answers. You will be expected to understand what you read, highlight the key parts of the text, interpret the underlying meanings, provide evidence in your responses, and explain how this evidence supports your main points. By using the testing strategies in the following section, you should be able to complete the constructed-response tasks effectively and successfully.

Testing Strategies that Work

1. Review the major parts of the constructed-response section—the questions and then the passage. Read *all* of the questions before you read the whole passage. This will give you an idea of what is being asked. It will also give you something to look for when reading the passage. Be sure that you understand what is being asked. At this point, you may not understand all of the questions because

you have not read the passage yet, but at least you will have an idea of what is expected of you. Next, review the passage. Look for boldfaced or italicized words, headings, or anything else that is easy to read. This quick survey will help you get familiar with the main ideas before you read the passage.

2. It is time to use the P.I.E.E. strategy that will help you with the constructed-response and any other written response sections included in the SBAC test. The P.I.E.E. strategy will help you think about the passages and questions in this section in a meaningful way. The letters in P.I.E.E. stand for *paraphrasing*, *interpreting*, *evidence-based*, and *explanatory*. The first two—*paraphrasing* and *interpreting*—are used during and after the reading of the passage. The last two—*evidence-based* and *explanatory*—describe a successful response. We will cover the first two, and then we will look at the last two when we are ready to construct our response. We will practice this strategy throughout this chapter, and there will be some chances for you to try this out on various passages.

3. After reading the passage the first time, take some notes on the notepad provided for you on the SBAC test. Get used to taking notes. This will help you when it comes time to construct a response. It is likely that you will use some exact words from your notes. This is like the prewriting part of the writing process, but it is faster. The "P" stands for *paraphrasing*, which is a shorter form of summarizing. It is recommended that you use bullet points like this:

> P.I.E.E. stands for a strategy.
> Paraphrasing and interpreting are used during and after reading.
> Evidence-based and explanatory describe a successful response.

Paraphrasing helps you think about the most important parts of the passage, and it also helps you focus on the important details of the passage. Since you are paraphrasing, or stating the main points in your own words, you are already critically thinking about what you have read. Paraphrasing can also help you organize your thoughts as you get ready to construct a response.

4. After reading the passage and after paraphrasing the important parts, you will interpret what you have read. When you interpret, you are trying to explain the deeper meaning that the author is trying to tell you in the passage. Ask yourself these questions:

> Why did the author write this passage?
> What is the theme or moral of this passage?
> What lesson does anyone learn in this passage?
> What is the purpose of this passage?

Asking these questions and answering them will guide you toward interpreting the reading passage. Again, creating bullet points in the notepad provided for you is important. The bullet points during the paraphrasing and interpreting parts of this strategy will help you with the last two parts of P.I.E.E. Interpreting text requires higher order thinking skills such as critical thinking and analysis. Use bullet points like this:

> The author wrote this chapter to inform the reader of useful strategies.
> The theme is to respond with critical and analytical interpretations.
> The purpose of this chapter is to improve test-taking skills.

5. Reread the passage and questions. At this point, you have paraphrased and interpreted the passage. Now you need to understand what the questions are asking you. We will practice this with sample passages later in the chapter. Chances are good that you will have answered the questions already just by paraphrasing and interpreting the passage.

6. You are now ready to write a response that should be described by the double "e" parts of P.I.E.E.—*evidence-based* and *explanatory*. It is important for your response to be evidence-based. This means that you cite text that is located in the passage to support your main points. If you make a point, provide evidence from the passage that proves that point. We will practice this a lot as we go through the practice test passages. Look through your paraphrasing notes. Was there evidence in those main points to support what you are now saying?

7. A successful constructed-response explains how this evidence supports your major points. Therefore, it is explanatory. Think about your notes when you interpreted the deeper meaning of the passage. How does your evidence support what you are saying? See how these parts of P.I.E.E. are connected? This will take practice, but you will succeed in writing an effective response if you use these strategies.

8. Finally, always reread your constructed-response for content and conventions. Is your content related to the question? Is it evidence-based and explanatory? Are you using grammatical conventions properly such as punctuation and capitalization?

Look at the following table. You may use this table while taking notes in your notepad.

Paraphrasing the main points or events.	Paraphrase here.
Interpreting the text.	Interpret here.
Evidence-based response provided.	Add evidence here.
Explanatory response provided.	Add explanations here.

Technology Effects on this Testing Section

Remember that this is a computer-adaptive test. Be sure that you are answering the questions with meaningful responses that focus on one main topic. You will have a notepad that you should get used to using for all constructed-response sections of the SBAC test. Also, remember that you must type your response in the space provided for you. Remember to cover all parts of the questions with evidence-based and explanatory responses. If it helps, use the practice passages and test questions from this book, but respond to the questions on a computer. This may help you practice the thinking process that goes with computer-based tests. Remember that more practice means that you are more prepared.

Although the scoring will depend on the specific questions being asked, the constructed-responses are based on a 2-point rubric. You may receive a 2, 1, or 0. Please look at the following guidelines below.

Rubric Guidelines for the Constructed-Response Section

2 Points	• The response provides enough evidence to support claims about the central idea. • There are specific examples from the passage that refer to the text. • The author's message is clearly stated and evidence-based.
1 Point	• There is limited evidence provided in the response that demonstrates understanding of the central idea. • The response has limited examples from the passage. • The response contains limited information that is evidence-based.
0 Points	• The response provides no evidence that supports a central idea. • There are no examples from the passage to support claims. • The response gives a possible central idea, but there is no explanation or information from the text.

CONSTRUCTED-RESPONSE TESTING PRACTICE

This section of the chapter is a place for practice. As a middle school student, you are asked to respond to questions that include a demonstration of deep meaning. This takes practice. Follow and practice the testing strategies that you have just read about including the P.I.E.E. strategies. There will be practice passages, practice questions, practice tables for you to use unless you are practicing on the computer, and sample practice responses. You will get better at this the more you practice using these strategies. Then you will be asked to practice on your own. Let's begin!

Passage 1—Narrative Passage

Directions: Read the following narrative passage below. Use the P.I.E.E. strategies that you have learned about in the previous section. You will be asked to write a constructed-response for some questions that follow the passage. Think about how to apply all strategies in order to answer the questions effectively.

A Tale of Two Cities
by Charles Dickens

Book 1—Recalled To Life

Chapter 1—The Period

IT WAS the best of times, it was the worst of times, it was the age of wisdom, it was the age of foolishness, it was the epoch of belief, it was the epoch of incredulity, it was the season of Light, it was the season of Darkness, it was the spring of hope, it was the winter of despair, we had everything before us, we had nothing before us, we were all going direct to Heaven, we were all going direct the other way—in short, the period was so far like the present period, that some of its noisiest authorities insisted on its being received, for good or for evil, in the superlative degree of comparison only.

There were a king with a large jaw and a queen with a plain face, on the throne of England; there were a king with a large jaw and a queen with a fair face, on the throne of France. In both countries it was clearer than crystal to the lords of the State preserves of loaves and fishes, that things in general were settled for ever.

It was the year of Our Lord one thousand seven hundred and seventy-five. Spiritual revelations were conceded to England at that favoured period, as at this. Mrs. Southcott had recently attained her five-and-twentieth blessed birth-day, of whom a prophetic private in the Life Guards had heralded the sublime appearance by announcing that arrangements were made for the swallowing up of London and Westminster. Even the Cock-lane ghost had been laid only a round dozen of years, after rapping out its messages, as the spirits of this very year last past (supernaturally deficient in originality) rapped out theirs. Mere messages in the earthly order of events had lately come to the English Crown and People, from a congress of British subjects in America: which, strange to relate, have proved more important to the human race than any communications yet received through any of the chickens of the Cock-lane brood.

1. What is the theme of this narrative? Support your chosen theme with textual evidence from the passage.

Apply All Strategies:

This question is looking to see how well you can interpret the narrative. You must provide a focused theme which illustrates the overall, underlying meaning that the author is trying to communicate to you. Usually focusing on what the character learns leads to the theme. The question asks that you infer what the message is of the narrative. This means that it will not be directly stated. As long as you can support your theme with specific evidence from the passage, you will succeed in responding. Use the table below to take notes using the P.I.E.E. strategy.

Paraphrasing the main points or events.	
Interpreting the text.	
Evidence-based response provided.	
Explanatory response provided.	

Write your constructed-response here.

Possible Constructed-Responses:

	Response	Rationale
2 Points	The theme of the narrative passage is that there is a feeling of a sameness in the countries of England and France. Furthermore, there is a duality that exists in the cities where "it was the best of times" and "the worst of times." Here, the author suggests that there are good times for some while there are complications for others. Clearly, some people are having good experiences while others may be undergoing problematic lives.	This response addresses all parts of the question. It offers a theme and supports that theme with textual evidence that is embedded within the words of the student.

	Response	Rationale
1 Point	The theme is that there is a feeling of problems for some people which must be faced. The king and queen of both England and France are the same. Spirituality is important in England.	This response makes two statements of fact and only offers a theme. There is no textual evidence that specifically proves the theme.
0 Points	There is something similar going on in England and France, and it seems like the two countries have the same problem.	This response is a statement that only makes a comment about the main idea of the passage. There is no theme with no textual evidence to support that theme.

When You Don't Get It

There is a chance that you will find some questions challenging, especially the ones that make you think critically. Look at the following strategies that may help you work through this question.

1. **Always read the question, and see if you can paraphrase what it is asking.** For example, you might paraphrase this question as the following: "The question is asking me to find a possible message of the story."

2. **Identify and address all of the parts of the question.** In this case, you may identify that you have two tasks. The first task is to determine the theme or message of the story. The second task is to provide textual evidence that supports your theme. You must address both of these parts of the question in order to receive a score of "2."

3. **Use the following sentence frames to help structure your response and to guide yourself through the question.**

   > The author wants to communicate the message that…
   > The most important moral of the passage is that…

Vocabulary Check

Look at vocabulary that you may be unfamiliar with, and try to use context clues to find the possible meaning of the word. For example, you may not recognize the word "sublime," which means you need to look at surrounding sentences and phrases in the passage to determine the meaning. Look at the following excerpt from the passage you just read.

> "…the **sublime** appearance by announcing that arrangements were made for the swallowing up of London and Westminster. Even the Cock-lane ghost had been laid only a round dozen of years, after rapping out its messages, as the spirits of this very year last past (supernaturally deficient in originality) rapped out theirs."

– **Sublime:** There is a "Cock-lane ghost" and a mention of "spirits of this very year" with some type of supernatural presence. Sublime must mean something that is at a high level of spirituality.

You may not get the exact definition, but you can talk it out and look at the context clues around that sentence. Sublime means "elevated to a high level of spirituality" in this passage.

2. Write a possible thesis statement for the introduction of an analytical essay. Include the theme and three points that you will make to prove your claims. Use textual evidence from the passage to support your thesis statement.

Apply All Strategies:

This item is asking you to write a possible thesis statement that could be found in an essay. Understand that analytical essays on narratives usually include the theme in the thesis statement. Also notice that this question is building from the first question. When you write a thesis statement, you usually provide the title of the novel or story and the theme. Because you already paraphrased and interpreted in the first table for the first question of this passage, you need only write the evidence and explanations that support your theme and three points. Again, use the P.I.E.E. strategy. The table below can be used for your notes.

Evidence-based response provided.	
Explanatory response provided.	

Write your constructed-response here.

Possible Constructed-Responses:

	Response	Rationale
2 Points	In "A Tale of Two Cities," the narrator expresses how it was "the best of times" and "the worst of times" simultaneously, which leads the reader to believe that two different worlds exist depending on the people one is speaking of in the cities. The author demonstrates this through the duality comments in the first paragraph, through the statements about the monarchs in England and France, and through the description of spirituality in the last paragraph.	This response begins with a possible thesis statement that includes the theme of the story. Textual evidence is used throughout the response to provide support. The student writes three points that prove the proposed theme in the thesis statement.
1 Point	In "A Tale of Two Cities," the narrator talks about different lives that some people lead in the two countries of England and France. In England and France, the kings have "large jaws," and the queens are similar, too.	This response includes a possible theme in a thesis statement although it is simple. The three points are missing although there is some textual evidence.
0 Points	There are many people who are having a hard time.	This response does not provide a thesis statement, the three points, or textual evidence.

When You Don't Get It

There is a chance that you will find some questions challenging, especially the ones that make you think critically. Look at the following strategies that may help you work through this question.

1. **Always read the question, and see if you can paraphrase what it is asking.** For example, you might paraphrase this question as the following: "The question is asking me to write a thesis statement with three key points that prove my assertions."

2. **Identify and address all of the parts of the question.** There are three parts of the question that ask you to complete three tasks: writing a thesis statement, making three points that prove the claims, and providing textual evidence.

3. **Use the following sentence frames to help structure your response and to guide yourself through the question.**

   > The author expresses that…
   > The three points that prove the proposed theme are…
   > Some textual evidence that supports these claims is…

Vocabulary Check

Look at vocabulary that you may be unfamiliar with, and try to use context clues to find the possible meaning of the word. For example, you may look at the word "epoch" and not know what it means until you look at the words and phrases around it. Look at the following excerpt from the passage that you just read.

> "IT WAS the best of times, it was the worst of times, it was the age of wisdom, it was the age of foolishness, it was the epoch of belief, it was the **epoch** of incredulity, it was the season of Light, it was the season of Darkness…."

– **Epoch:** The author uses similar words in each set of phrases. Before "the epoch of belief," the author says that "it was the age of wisdom." Epoch may be similar to an age then.

By talking this out, you can make an educated guess about what the word means. The author does a lot of repetition in this section of the passage, so you are bound to see similarities among the phrases offered. An epoch is a period of time like an age in history in this passage.

Passage 2—Nonfiction Passage

Directions: Read the following nonfiction passage below. Use the P.I.E.E. strategies that you have learned about in the previous section. You will be asked to write a constructed-response for some questions that follow the passage. Think about how to apply all strategies in order to answer the questions effectively.

A Florida Sketch-Book
by Bradford Torrey

In approaching Jacksonville by rail, the traveler rides hour after hour through seemingly endless pine barrens, otherwise known as low pine-woods and flat-woods, till he wearies of the sight. It would be hard, he thinks, to imagine a region more unwholesome looking and uninteresting, more poverty-stricken and God-forsaken, in its entire aspect. Surely, men who would risk life in behalf of such a country deserved to win their cause.

Monotonous as the flat-woods were, however, and malarious as they looked,—arid wastes and stretches of stagnant water flying past the car window in perpetual alternation, I was impatient to get into them. They were a world the like of which I had never seen; and wherever I went in eastern Florida, I made it one of my earliest concerns to seek them out.

My first impression was one of disappointment, or perhaps I should rather say, of bewilderment. In fact, I returned from my first visit to the flat-woods under the delusion that I had not been into them at all. This was at St. Augustine, whither I had gone after a night only in Jacksonville. I looked about the quaint little city, of course, and went to the South Beach, on St. Anastasia Island; then I wished to see the pine lands. They were to be found, I was told, on the other side of the San Sebastian. The sun was hot (or so it seemed to a man fresh from the rigors of a New England winter), and the sand was deep; but I sauntered through New Augustine, and pushed on up the road toward Moultrie (I believe it was), till the last houses were passed and I came to the edge of the pine-woods. Here, presently, the roads began to fork in a very confusing manner. The first man I met—a kindly cracker— cautioned me against getting lost; but I had no thought of taking the slightest risk of that kind. I was not going to explore the woods, but only to enter them, sit down, look about me, and listen. The difficulty was to get into them. As I advanced, they receded. It was still only the beginning of a wood; the trees far apart and comparatively small, the ground covered thickly with saw palmetto, interspersed here and there with patches of brown grass or sedge.

In many places the roads were under water, and as I seemed to be making little progress, I pretty soon sat down in a pleasantly shaded spot. Wagons came along at intervals, all going toward the city, most of them with loads of wood; ridiculously small loads, such as a Yankee boy would put upon a wheelbarrow. "Fine day," said I to the driver of such a cart. "Yes, sir," he answered, "it's a pretty day." He spoke with an emphasis which seemed to imply that he accepted my remark as well meant, but hardly adequate to the occasion. Perhaps, if the day had been a few shades brighter, he would have called it "handsome," or even "good looking."

Expressions of this kind, however, are matters of local or individual taste, and as such are not to be disputed about. Thus, a man stopped me in Tallahassee to inquire what time it was. I told him, and he said, "Ah, a little sooner than I thought." And why not "sooner" as well as "earlier"? But when, on the same road, two white girls in an ox-cart hailed me with the question, "What time 't is?" I thought the interrogative idiom a little queer; almost as queer, shall we say, as "How do you do?" may have sounded to the first man who heard it,—if the reader is able to imagine such a person.

1. What is the central idea in this passage? Summarize the passage with details that support the central idea. Use evidence from the text to prove your assertions.

Apply All Strategies:

This item is asking you to determine what the deeper meaning of the passage is. What is the main point that the author is making? Look at the title of the article in order to get a hint about what the central idea is. Again, be sure to use evidence from the article to prove all of your points. Use the P.I.E.E. strategy and the table below to take notes before constructing a response.

Paraphrasing the main points or events.	
Interpreting the text.	
Evidence-based response provided.	
Explanatory response provided.	

Write your constructed-response here.

[blank response box]

Possible Constructed-Responses:

	Response	Rationale
2 Points	The central idea in this passage is that the flat-woods seem elusive, yet intriguing and interesting to the narrator. The "traveler rides hour after hour through seemingly endless pine barrens" just to reach a part of the state, so that he can get to the flat-woods. Furthermore, the author states that "they were a world the like of which he [I] had never seen" even though he initially claims that it is "monotonous." Clearly, there is something special about this place to the narrator.	This response states a clear central idea that represents the most important message of the passage. The student provides details in a summary that also adds textual evidence in the form of embedded quotes.

	Response	Rationale
1 Point	The narrator travels far and wide to get to the flat-woods, and the central idea is that the narrator actually likes the flat-woods. He was "impatient to get to them."	This response makes a statement, includes a central idea, and adds some textual evidence. However, the student does not provide an adequate summary with details that have textual evidence to support the claims.
0 Points	The narrator is traveling to a place which he likes.	This response is only a statement that vaguely suggests a central idea. There is no summary, and details supported by textual evidence are missing.

When You Don't Get It

There is a chance that you will find some questions challenging, especially the ones that make you think critically. Look at the following strategies that may help you work through this question.

1. **Always read the question, and see if you can paraphrase what it is asking.** For example, you might paraphrase the question as the following: "The question is asking me to write the most important idea of the passage, to write a summary with details that support the main idea, and to provide textual evidence that supports my claims."

2. **Identify and address all of the parts of the question.** There are four parts to this question that need to be addressed. There needs to be a central idea that is stated. There must be an adequate summary. This summary must include important details, and textual evidence should be provided to support all claims.

3. **Use the following sentence frames to help structure your response and to guide yourself through the question.**

   > The central idea, or big idea, of the passage is that…
   > A possible summary of the main idea and points of the passage is that…
   > Textual evidence that supports my claims is…

Vocabulary Check

Look at vocabulary that you may be unfamiliar with, and try to use context clues to find the possible meaning of the word. Look at the following excerpt from the passage.

"The difficulty was to get into them. As I advanced, they **receded**."

– **Receded:** The author says it is difficult to get to the flat-woods, so it makes sense that the word "receded" means go backward because the author advances, or goes forward, at first to try to get to the flat-woods.

2. The title of the passage is *A Florida Sketch-Book*. What is the author's purpose for writing this passage? Provide textual evidence to support your statements.

Apply All Strategies:

This item is asking you to figure out the reason why the author wrote this passage. What message is the author trying to communicate to the reader? Again, the title will clue you in to the author's purpose. Be sure to mention if the passage was written to persuade, to entertain, or to inform, as that is usually something that is expected when discussing an author's purpose. Use the second half of the P.I.E.E. table to take notes for this question.

Evidence-based response provided.	
Explanatory response provided.	

Write your constructed-response here.

```



```

Possible Constructed-Responses:

	Response	Rationale
2 Points	The author's purpose for writing this passage is to inform the reader about the life of a part of the state of Florida that clearly beckons him and that has a rich culture other places may not have. General information is included such as how to get there and what types of places lead to the flat-woods such as "...the South Beach, on St. Anastasia Island; then he [I] wished to see the pine lands. They were to be found, he [I] was told, on the other side of the San Sebastian." Again, the narrator suggests how special the flat-woods are when he says his primary goal is "to enter them, sit down, look about me, and listen."	This response clearly states that the purpose of this author is to inform the reader by providing facts and by commenting on the most important idea in the passage. It includes information that proves the main idea suggested, and it adds textual evidence to support the student's claims.

	Response	Rationale
1 Point	The author tells the reader about the ways to get to the flat-woods in Florida and describes the areas that lead to this place. In fact, he "makes it one of his [my] earliest concerns to seek them out."	This response suggests a central idea with some details and textual evidence. However, the student does not include the author's purpose for writing the passage.
0 Points	The author explains a lot about areas in Eastern Florida.	This response offers a main idea, but does not provide the author's purpose for writing the passage. This response also does not include textual evidence.

When You Don't Get It

There is a chance that you will find some questions challenging, especially the ones that make you think critically. Look at the following strategies that may help you work through this question.

1. **Always read the question, and see if you can paraphrase what it is asking.** For example, you might paraphrase this question as the following: "The question is asking me to state the author's purpose for writing the passage and to support my claims."

2. **Identify and address all of the parts of the question.** There are two key parts to this question. First, the response should include why the author wrote the passage. The second part is including textual evidence to support the statements that prove the proposed author's purpose is accurate.

3. **Use the following sentence frames to help structure your response and to guide yourself through the question.**

   > The author wrote this passage because he/she wanted to...
   > Textual evidence that supports the author's purpose is...

Vocabulary Check

Look at vocabulary that you may be unfamiliar with, and try to use context clues to find the possible meaning of the word. Look at the following excerpt from the passage. Look at how you might talk this out to make sense of the vocabulary word in question.

> "…It was still only the beginning of a wood; the trees far apart and comparatively small, the ground covered thickly with saw palmetto, **interspersed** here and there with patches of brown grass or sedge…."

– **Interspersed:** The author says that the ground is "covered thickly" to explain how the "patches of brown grass or sedge" is different. Thus, "interspersed here and there" must mean spotted across the area. In this passage, interspersed means "scattered here and there."

Passage 3—Narrative Passage

Directions: Read the following narrative passage below. Use the P.I.E.E. strategies that you have learned about in the previous section. You will be asked to write a constructed-response for some questions that follow the passage. Think about how to apply all strategies in order to answer the questions effectively.

Metamorphosis
by Franz Kafka

One morning, when Gregor Samsa woke from troubled dreams, he found himself transformed in his bed into a horrible vermin. He lay on his armour-like back, and if he lifted his head a little he could see his brown belly, slightly domed and divided by arches into stiff sections. The bedding was hardly able to cover it and seemed ready to slide off any moment. His many legs, pitifully thin compared with the size of the rest of him, waved about helplessly as he looked.

"What's happened to me?" he thought. It wasn't a dream. His room, a proper human room although a little too small, lay peacefully between its four familiar walls. A collection of textile samples lay spread out on the table—Samsa was a travelling salesman—and above it there hung a picture that he had recently cut out of an illustrated magazine and housed in a nice, gilded frame. It showed a lady fitted out with a fur hat and fur boa who sat upright, raising a heavy fur muff that covered the whole of her lower arm towards the viewer.

Gregor then turned to look out the window at the dull weather. Drops of rain could be heard hitting the pane, which made him feel quite sad. "How about if I sleep a little bit longer and forget all this nonsense," he thought, but that was something he was unable to do because he was used to sleeping on his right, and in his present state couldn't get into that position. However hard he threw himself onto his right, he always rolled back to where he was. He must have tried it a hundred times, shut his eyes so that he wouldn't have to look at the floundering legs, and only stopped when he began to feel a mild, dull pain there that he had never felt before.

"Oh, God," he thought, "what a strenuous career it is that I've chosen! Travelling day in and day out. Doing business like this takes much more effort than doing your own business at home, and on top of that there's the curse of travelling, worries about making train connections, bad and irregular food, contact with different people all the time so that you can never get to know anyone or become friendly with them…" He felt a slight itch up on his belly; pushed himself slowly up on his back towards the headboard so that he could lift his head better; found where the itch was, and saw that it was covered with lots of little white spots which he didn't know what to make of; and when he tried to feel the place with one of his legs he drew it quickly back because as soon as he touched it he was overcome by a cold shudder.

He slid back into his former position. "Getting up early all the time," he thought, "it makes you stupid. You've got to get enough sleep. Other travelling salesmen live a life of luxury. For instance, whenever I go back to the guest house during the morning to copy out the contract, these gentlemen are always still sitting there eating their breakfasts. I ought to just try that with my boss; I'd get kicked out on the spot. But who knows, maybe that would be the best thing for me. If I didn't have my parents to think about I'd have given in my notice a long time ago, I'd have gone up to the boss and told him just what I think, tell him everything I would, let him know just what I feel. He'd fall right off his desk! And it's a funny sort of business to be sitting up there at your desk, talking down at your subordinates from up there, especially when you have to go right up close because the boss is hard of hearing. Well, there's still some hope; once I've got the money together to pay off my parents' debt to him—another five or six years I suppose—that's definitely what I'll do. That's when I'll make the big change. First of all though, I've got to get up, my train leaves at five."

1. What is the setting of this fictional narrative? How does it contribute to the development of the plot structure and story?

Apply All Strategies:

This question is looking to see how well you can interpret the narrative and how well you can explain the role of an identified setting and its effect on the plot structure and development. Think about the main parts of a plot structure, and determine where the setting would appear. Then establish how the setting sets the stage for the rest of the story. Use the P.I.E.E. strategies to begin your brainstorming session prior to writing your constructed-response.

Paraphrasing the main points or events.	
Interpreting the text.	
Evidence-based response provided.	
Explanatory response provided.	

Write your constructed-response here.

Possible Constructed-Responses:

	Response	Rationale
2 Points	The setting immediately begins with the development of the plot because the character finds himself "transformed in his bed into a horrible vermin." The setting is part of the exposition in a general plot structure diagram, and it begins the development of the narrative because it advances the plot events forward by introducing the main conflict in this story.	This response addresses all parts of the question. It offers a possible setting, discusses where in the plot structure setting occurs, and traces the development of the narrative based on the setting. It also embeds textual evidence from the text to support the student's claims and assertions.

	Response	Rationale
1 Point	The setting of this narrative is where the setting takes place and what is happening in the story. A man becomes a "vermin" and must deal with this problem.	This response explains how the setting in the story is related to the definition of a setting with one word cited from the text. It suggests that there is a problem, but it does not discuss how the setting develops the plot structure or narrative.
0 Points	A man turns into something bad, and he wants to be different and back to his human form.	This response summarizes the setting, but does not address all parts of the question. It also does not provide textual evidence to support the student's claims.

When You Don't Get It

There is a chance that you will find some questions challenging, especially the ones that make you think critically. Look at the following strategies that may help you work through this question.

1. **Always read the question, and see if you can paraphrase what it is asking.** For example, you might paraphrase this question as the following: "The question is asking me to identify where the story takes place and discuss how it contributes to the plot structure and development of the narrative."

2. **Identify and address all of the parts of the question.** In this case, you may identify that you have two tasks. The first task is to determine the setting. The second task is to explain how it affects the development of plot structure and of the story. You need to know the basic stages of plot structure in order to respond to this question effectively. Plot structure is made up of the exposition, the rising action, the climax, the falling action, and the resolution. Knowledge of this information is important because it is required in order to address all parts of the question.

3. **Use the following sentence frames to help structure your response and to guide yourself through the question.**

> ➤ The setting of the narrative is…
> ➤ The setting contributes to the development of the plot structure and story by…

Vocabulary Check

Look at vocabulary that you may be unfamiliar with, and try to use context clues to find the possible meaning of the word. For example, an important word to understand is "vermin." Read the excerpt from this passage, and use context clues to determine the meaning of the word.

> "One morning, when Gregor Samsa woke from troubled dreams, he found himself transformed in his bed into a horrible **vermin**. He lay on his armour-like back, and if he lifted his head a little he could see his brown belly, slightly domed and divided by arches into stiff sections…."

– **Vermin:** The author uses the word "horrible" before vermin, so it must be something extremely negative. Also, the sentence following "vermin" describes Gregor as having an "armour-like back" with "stiff sections," so it sounds like he has turned into some type of insect.

You may not get the exact definition, but you can talk it out and look at the context clues around that sentence. Vermin means "a type of pest" in this passage.

2. What is the point of view used in this passage? How does it impact the development of the main character, or protagonist?

Apply All Strategies:

This item is asking you to identify the point of view used in this passage by Kafka. Authors are very careful about the type of point of view that they select for a fictional narrative. Think about how the point of view helps the reader to understand the story better. What do you learn about Gregor that increases your interpretation of his character? Again, use the P.I.E.E. strategy. The table below can be used for your notes.

Evidence-based response provided.	
Explanatory response provided.	

Write your constructed-response here.

Possible Constructed-Responses:

	Response	Rationale
2 Points	Kafka utilizes third person point of view which means that he is using a narration that relates the feeling and thoughts of the characters throughout the story using pronouns such as "he, she, and they." Kafka opens the narrative with the shocking thoughts of his main character, Gregor. We learn that Gregor "was a travelling salesman" who seems unhappy with his lot as he states that he wishes he could make "the big change." Ironically, he has changed, and these insights of his character match his predicament.	This response identifies the point of view used accurately and describes what this point of view utilizes when in use by an author. This response also delves into the character of Gregor and points out how his situation is ironic as it matches the precise circumstance in which Gregor finds himself. The development of the character, or protagonist, is clear in this response.
1 Point	Kafka uses third person point of view. The main character is surprised by his transformation into "vermin," and he is trying to understand his situation.	This response includes the type of point of view that is used by Kafka and summarizes the setting with one word cited. However, this response does not explain the effect of this point of view on the development of the main character, or protagonist.
0 Points	Gregor is the main character and becomes a horrible creature. Gregor tells us about this main event in his life.	This response explains what has happened to the main character; however, it does not identify the point of view, and it does not demonstrate how it further develops the main character.

When You Don't Get It

There is a chance that you will find some questions challenging, especially the ones that make you think critically. Look at the following strategies that may help you work through this question.

1. **Always read the question, and see if you can paraphrase what it is asking.** For example, you might paraphrase this question as the following: "The question is asking me to identify the point of view. I should explain how this point of view is used, and I should also describe how it affects the development of the main character, or protagonist."

2. **Identify and address all of the parts of the question.** There are two main parts to this question. First, you must state the point of view and explain how it is used by the author. Second, you need to explain how it impacts the development of the main character. Look at what you learn about Gregor as the story moves forward.

3. **Use the following sentence frames to help structure your response and to guide yourself through the question.**

   > The author uses the type of point of view which…
   > The point of view contributes to the development of the character by…

Vocabulary Check

Look at vocabulary that you may be unfamiliar with, and try to use context clues to find the possible meaning of the word. For example, you may look at the word "strenuous" and not know what it means until you look at the words and phrases around it. Look at the following excerpt from the passage that you just read.

> "Oh, God," he thought, "what a **strenuous** career it is that I've chosen! Travelling day in and day out. Doing business like this takes much more effort than doing your own business at home, and on top of that there's the curse of travelling, worries about making train connections, bad and irregular food, contact with different people all the time so that you can never get to know anyone or become friendly with them…."

– **Strenuous:** Gregor thinks about this "strenuous career" that he has chosen. The sentences following the sentence with the word "strenuous" describe traveling every day and putting a lot of "effort" into traveling conditions and procedures. It seems that strenuous means "really hard."

Looking at surrounding phrases and sentences is a good way to determine the meaning of an unknown word. There will almost always be context clues around the unknown word, so try to recognize those clues. Make it a habit to look for these clues whenever you come across a word that you do not know. In this passage, strenuous means "using a lot of energy that makes one exhausted."

Passage 4—Narrative Passage

Directions: Read the following narrative passage below. Use the P.I.E.E. strategies that you have learned about in the previous section. You will be asked to write a constructed-response for some questions that follow the passage. Think about how to apply all strategies in order to answer the questions effectively.

A Dog's Tale
by Mark Twain

My father was a St. Bernard, my mother was a collie, but I am a Presbyterian. This is what my mother told me, I do not know these nice distinctions myself. To me they are only fine large words meaning nothing. My mother had a fondness for such; she liked to say them, and see other dogs look surprised and envious, as wondering how she got so much education. But, indeed, it was not real education; it was only show: she got the words by listening in the dining-room and drawing-room when there was company, and by going with the children to Sunday-school and listening there; and whenever she heard a large word she said it over to herself many times, and so was able to keep it until there was a dogmatic gathering in the neighborhood, then she would get it off, and surprise and distress them all, from pocket-pup to mastiff, which rewarded her for all her trouble. If there was a stranger he was nearly sure to be suspicious, and when he got his breath again he would ask her what it meant. And she always told him. He was never expecting this but thought he would catch her; so when she told him, he was the one that looked ashamed, whereas he had thought it was going to be she. The others were always waiting for this, and glad of it and proud of her, for they knew what was going to happen, because they had had experience. When she told the meaning of a big word they were all so taken up with admiration that it never occurred to any dog to doubt if it was the right one; and that was natural, because, for one thing, she answered up so promptly that it seemed like a dictionary speaking, and for another thing, where could they find out whether it was right or not? for she was the only cultivated dog there was. By and by, when I was older, she brought home the word Unintellectual, one time, and worked it pretty hard all the week at different gatherings, making much unhappiness and despondency; and it was at this time that I noticed that during that week she was asked for the meaning at eight different assemblages, and flashed out a fresh definition every time, which showed me that she had more presence of mind than culture, though I said nothing, of course. She had one word which she always kept on hand, and ready, like a life-preserver, a kind of emergency word to strap on when she was likely to get washed overboard in a sudden way—that was the word Synonymous. When she happened to fetch out a long word which had had its day weeks before and its prepared meanings gone to her dump-pile, if there was a stranger there of course it knocked him groggy for a couple of minutes, then he would come to, and by that time she would be away down wind on another tack, and not expecting anything; so when he'd hail and ask her to cash in, I (the only dog on the inside of her game) could see her canvas flicker a moment— but only just a moment—then it would belly out taut and full, and she would say, as calm as a summer's day, "It's synonymous with supererogation," or some godless long reptile of a word like that, and go placidly about and skim away on the next tack, perfectly comfortable, you know, and leave that stranger looking profane and embarrassed, and the initiated slatting the floor with their tails in unison and their faces transfigured with a holy joy.

1. How is personification used in this passage? Predict how personification may be used to affect the theme in this excerpt from a short story.

Apply All Strategies:

This question is looking to see how well you can interpret the narrative and how well you can explain the role of an identified setting and its effect on the plot structure and development. Think about the main parts of a plot structure, and determine where the setting would appear. Then establish how the setting sets the stage for the rest of the story. Use the P.I.E.E. strategies to begin your brainstorming session prior to writing your constructed-response.

Paraphrasing the main points or events.	
Interpreting the text.	
Evidence-based response provided.	
Explanatory response provided.	

Write your constructed-response here.

Possible Constructed-Responses:

	Response	Rationale
2 Points	The dog is personified in this short story. Personification is used in order to give human qualities to an object or animal to emphasize something or to make a point. I predict that the dog is being personified because it will be likened to the spirit of a human being in the end.	This response answers the first question, which asks how personification is used. This response clarifies that the dog is personified. This response also includes a possible effect of personification on the theme which is not yet known based on this passage.
1 Point	Personification means that a thing is given human qualities. The narrator is personified, which might mean that the dog is really a human.	This response defines personification and implies that the dog is personified. There is no clear prediction of how personification is used to affect the theme.
0 Points	Personification is when a thing has human characteristics.	This response only defines personification and does not answer either question.

When You Don't Get It

There is a chance that you will find some questions challenging, especially the ones that make you think critically. Look at the following strategies that may help you work through this question.

1. **Always read the question, and see if you can paraphrase what it is asking.** For example, you might paraphrase this question as the following: "The question is asking how personification is used in this passage, so I need to explain how the dog is being personified. The second question asks me to predict how this use of personification could affect the theme."

2. **Identify and address all of the parts of the question.** In this case, you may identify that you have two tasks. The first task is to identify how personification is used in this passage. You must know the definition of personification before you can answer this question. You may recall that personification is used to give inanimate objects or animals human qualities. You must then realize that the dog is being personified. The last question asks you to predict how this use of personification may affect the theme. This takes interpretation of the text. Go back to your P.I.E.E. chart to see what your interpretations were before responding to this question.

3. **Use the following sentence frames to help structure your response and to guide through the question.**

   > The object or animal being personified in this passage is the…
   > A possible theme involving personification is…

Vocabulary Check

Look at vocabulary that you may be unfamiliar with, and try to use context clues to find the possible meaning of the word. For example, an important word to understand is the word "distinctions." Read the excerpt from this passage, and use context clues to determine the meaning of the word.

> "My father was a St. Bernard, my mother was a collie, but I am a Presbyterian. This is what my mother told me, I do not know these nice **distinctions** myself. To me they are only fine large words meaning nothing. My mother had a fondness for such; she liked to say them, and see other dogs look surprised and envious, as wondering how she got so much education."

– **Distinctions:** The narrator makes an interesting opening comment and states that his/her mother told him/her this even if the "distinctions" are not understood. Distinctions must mean the differences among those three words—St. Bernard, collie, and Presbyterian.

You may not get the exact definition, but you can talk it out and look at the context clues around that sentence. Distinctions means "differences among things."

2. Why does the narrator speak of knowledge of words and vocabulary? What is a possible theme of this passage?

Apply All Strategies:

This item is asking you to create a possible theme of this passage and is followed by a question about a possible focus on the words and vocabulary comments of the narrator. Use your P.I.E.E. chart to write down evidence and explanations that may help you respond to this question.

Evidence-based response provided.	
Explanatory response provided.	

Write your constructed-response here.

Possible Constructed-Responses:

	Response	Rationale
2 Points	The narrator discusses his/her mother's obsession with knowing words and using these words to impress other dogs. This leads me to believe that a possible theme is that humans can be trivial and possibly petty.	This response explains why the narrator is talking about using impressive vocabulary words. It also provides a possible theme that can be interpreted based on the information thus given in this excerpt.
1 Point	The narrator talks about his/her mother's interest in knowing words and using them to get attention from the other dogs because he/she may find it hard to understand why this was a preoccupation of his/her mother.	This response answers the first question quite well; however, there is no possible theme provided, so only partial credit is given for this response.
0 Points	Dogs like to use a lot of hard vocabulary in this passage.	This response taps into the difficulty of the mother's vocabulary; however, neither question is addressed or answered.

When You Don't Get It

There is a chance that you will find some questions challenging, especially the ones that make you think critically. Look at the following strategies that may help you work through this question.

1. **Always read the question, and see if you can paraphrase what it is asking.** For example, you might paraphrase this question as the following: "The question is asking me to give a reason why the narrator is spending time talking about vocabulary. The second question asks for a possible theme of this passage based on what information is given to me."

2. **Identify and address all of the parts of the question.** There are two main parts to this question. First, you must discuss why the narrator talks about his/her mother's preoccupation with knowing vocabulary words to impress and possibly to intimidate other dogs. Think about plausible reasons for this. The second question is asking you to form a possible theme of this passage. This takes interpretation. Refer to your P.I.E.E. chart for this passage.

3. **Use the following sentence frames to help structure your response and to guide yourself through the question.**

   > The narrator talks a lot about his/her mother who likes to use hard vocabulary because…
   > A possible theme based on this passage is that…

Vocabulary Check

Look at vocabulary that you may be unfamiliar with, and try to use context clues to find the possible meaning of the word. For example, you may look at the word "dogmatic" and not know what it means until you look at the words and phrases around it. Look at the following excerpt from the passage that you just read.

> "…and whenever she heard a large word she said it over to herself many times, and so was able to keep it until there was a **dogmatic** gathering in the neighborhood, then she would get it off, and surprise and distress them all, from pocket-pup to mastiff, which rewarded her for all her trouble…."

– **Dogmatic:** When there was a "dogmatic gathering," the narrator's mother "would get it off" and be impassioned with her vocabulary usage which must mean that the gathering is very opinionated and intense.

Looking at surrounding phrases and sentences is a good way to determine the meaning of an unknown word. There will almost always be context clues around the unknown word, so try to recognize those clues. Make it a habit to look for these clues whenever you come across a word that you do not know. In this passage, dogmatic means "with great emphasis and intensity."

On Your Own

Passage 5—Nonfiction Passage

Directions: Read the following nonfiction passage below. Use the P.I.E.E. strategies that you have learned about in the previous section. You will be asked to write a constructed-response for some questions that follow the passage. Think about how to apply all strategies in order to answer the questions effectively.

What I Saw in California
by Edwin Bryant

"All which I saw, and part of which I was." –Dryden

...The district of country known geographically as Upper California is bounded on the north by Oregon, the forty-second degree of north latitude being the boundary line between the two territories; on the east by the Rocky Mountains and the Sierra de los Mimbres, a continuation of the same range; on the south by Sonora and Old or Lower California, and on the west by the Pacific Ocean...

The largest river of Upper California is the Colorado or Red, which has a course of about 1000 miles, and empties into the Gulf of California in latitude about 32 degrees north. But little is known of the region through which this stream flows. The report of trappers, however, is that the river is *canoned* between high mountains and precipices a large portion of its course, and that its banks and the country generally through which it flows are arid, sandy, and barren. Green and Grand Rivers are its principal upper tributaries, both of which rise in the Rocky Mountains, and within the territories of the United States. The Gila is its lowest and largest branch, emptying into the Colorado, just above its mouth. Sevier and Virgin Rivers are also tributaries of the Colorado. Mary's River rises near latitude 42 degrees north, and has a course of about 400 miles, when its waters sink in the sands of the desert. This river is not laid down on any map which I have seen. The Sacramento and San Joaquin Rivers have each a course of from 300 to 400 miles, the first flowing from the north and the last from the south, and both emptying into the Bay of St. Francisco at the same point. They water the large and fertile valley lying between the Sierra Nevada and the coast range of mountains. I subjoin a description of the valley and river San Joaquin, from the pen of a gentleman (Dr. Marsh) who has explored the river from its source to its mouth.

"This noble valley is the first undoubtedly in California, and one of the most magnificent in the world. It is about 500 miles long, with an-average width of about fifty miles. It is bounded on the east by the great Snowy Mountains, and on the west by the low range, which in many places dwindles into insignificant hills, and has its northern terminus at the Strait of Carquines, on the Bay of San Francisco, and its southern near the Colorado River.

"The river of San Joaquin flows through the middle of the valley for about half of its extent, and thence diverges towards the eastern mountain, in which it has its source. About sixty miles further south is the northern end of the Buena Vista Lake, which is about one hundred miles long, and from ten to twenty wide. Still farther south, and near the western side of the valley, is another and much smaller lake.

"The great lake receives about a dozen tributaries on its eastern side, which all rise in the great range of the Snowy Mountains. Some of these streams flow through broad and fertile valleys within the mountain's range, and, from thence emerging, irrigate the plains of the great valley for the distance of twenty or thirty miles. The largest of these rivers is called by the Spanish inhabitants the river Reyes, and falls into the lake near its northern end; it is a well-timbered stream, and flows through a country of great fertility and beauty. The tributaries of the San Joaquin are all on the east side.

"On ascending the stream we first meet with the Stanislaus, a clear rapid mountain stream, some forty or fifty yards wide, with a considerable depth of water in its lower portion. The Mormons have commenced a settlement, called New Hope, and built some two or three houses near the mouth.

"There are considerable bodies of fertile land along the river, and the higher plains afford good pasturage…

"In the valleys of the rivers which come down from the great Snowy Mountains are vast bodies of pine, and red-wood, or cedar timber, and the streams afford water power to any desirable amount.

"The whole country east of the San Joaquin, and the water communication which connects it with the lakes, is considered, by the best judges, to be particularly adapted to the culture of the vine, which must necessarily become one of the principal agricultural resources of California."

1. The opening quote by Dryden introduces the description of California. What does it mean? How does it relate to the central message of the passage? Support your assertions with textual evidence from the passage.

   Write your constructed-response here or on a computer.

2. What is the purpose of the author's inclusion of Dr. Marsh's description of California? Cite textual evidence that supports your claims.

   Write your constructed-response here or on a computer.

3. Think about the reasons why the author wrote this nonfiction piece about the state of California. What is the underlying meaning of this passage? This means that there is a type of deeper meaning that the author is trying to communicate to you. Cite textual evidence to support your claims and assertions.

Write your constructed-response here or on a computer.

(Answers are on pages 151–152.)

Remember to:

> Review the questions and key features of the passage such as italicized words or titles.
> Understand what is being asked for an effective constructed-response.
> Use the P.I.E.E. strategy, and take notes.

Performance Task (PT)

Understanding the Performance Task Section

The SBAC test includes the Computer-Adaptive Test (CAT) and a Performance Task (PT) that is part of the SBAC testing schedule for seventh grade ELA. The Performance Task includes three components—a classroom activity, ELA PT Part 1, and ELA PT Part 2. The classroom activity is guided by the teacher prior to the testing sessions. The classroom activity is designed to familiarize the student with vocabulary or context that may help students in thinking about the Performance Task. More on the classroom activity will follow in the "Connecting the Classroom Activity to the PT" section of this chapter.

Two hours are allotted for the Performance Task (both parts). Thirty minutes is the approximate time suggested for the classroom activity which precedes the two parts. Students are allowed to take breaks; however, they will be logged out if the test is paused for more than twenty minutes. There are two options for taking notes for both of the Performance Task parts. Students may use global notes which enable students to take notes on the computer. They may also opt to take notes with scratch paper that they write on. Either way, the student can access the notes during ELA PT Part 2 at any time including the notes generated from ELA PT Part 1.

The Performance Task has a purpose of asking students to dig deeper in order to respond to questions that are more complex within a common topic or issue. The Performance Task seeks to measure how students can use what they have learned over the course of the school year to answer questions that cover numerous claims as described in the first chapter. The focus is having students demonstrate their ability to take their knowledge and skill sets and to apply that to a challenging, real-world topic or issue. Critical thinking, analytical skills, research and writing abilities, and citing of evidence are all key components needed in order to respond to both parts successfully.

Students are asked to do two primary actions during the Performance Task— to read and understand research and to write. Students will need to be able to integrate these two skills in order to complete the Performance Task to meet high expectations. They will be asked to write an explanatory text, an argumentative essay, or a narrative. All of these performance task rubrics are included in the appendix of this book. They are similar to the writing rubrics, but they are different. Be sure that the rubrics say, "Performance Task Writing Rubric." Students will need to demonstrate their ability to extend knowledge and skills while working with multiple informational sources and research articles.

Connecting the Classroom Activity to the PT

The classroom activity is run by the classroom teacher at least one to three days before the Performance Task test. Your entire seventh grade class will participate in the classroom activity together. It is approximately 30 minutes in length, and it is not scored. The classroom activity will be completed on a separate day than the actual Performance Task test. The classroom activity is meant to familiarize students with the context of the Performance Task, so that all students have an equitable chance of doing well on the actual test. This includes support in understanding the setting or situation included in the Performance Task or in learning key vocabulary and terminology used specifically in the Performance Task.

During a typical classroom activity, students will be exposed to images, examples, or informational reading that will help bring context to the setting or situation specific to the Performance Task. Students will also be asked to engage in a classroom discussion to work together in understanding the context more fully. This will be a structured discussion led by the classroom teacher. It is important for students to pay attention during this part of the Performance Task as it can provide necessary support for students who have less experience with the topic or situation. Key concepts and vocabulary may also help students in responding to questions and to writing prompts successfully.

To maximize the classroom activity, it will be important that students pay close attention to anything that they are unfamiliar with, whether that be key concepts, vocabulary words, or contextual details. The whole point of the classroom activity is to level the playing field. This means that no student should have an advantage over another student just because their prior experiences are different. The class discussion can also help students begin thinking about the main topic or issue. It is done on a separate day of the test in order for students to have some time to think about the important ideas that are included in the Performance Task.

The best way to connect the classroom activity to the actual Performance Task test is to participate in the discussion, to familiarize oneself with the key concepts and unknown vocabulary, and to begin thinking about the topic, issue, or situation presented during the classroom activity. This will prepare students adequately for the next part, which is to work independently on research and on writing activities of the Performance Task.

Testing Strategies that Work

1. As stated in the previous section, it is important that you pay close attention to the topics, issues, concepts, and vocabulary presented in the classroom activity. This sets the stage for the Performance Task test. If anything is unknown or unfamiliar, ask questions. This time is allotted for you to explore the ideas and terminology that will be used in the Performance Task, so that you will not need to worry about that as you maneuver through the research articles and informational sources. Also, be sure to participate in the classroom activity discussions. This is a good time to collaborate with classmates to really begin thinking about the topic or problem presented.

2. Review all of the sections of the Performance Task before you begin reading more thoroughly. Look at the headings, the format of the test, and the information provided. Familiarize yourself with all of the information that is given, so that you understand how the test is organized and what content is included. Once you have done this, then you will be able to read everything more carefully with an eye toward the more comprehensive details.

3. Pay attention to the writing genre that will be assigned for this Performance Task in ELA PT Part 2. You will be given an argumentative writing piece, an explanatory writing task, or a narrative. Determine this before you read the sources carefully and before you take notes. Begin planning how you might want to approach the writing task. Do you know what your position or claim will be if it is an argumentative writing task? Once you know your position, you will be able to take notes with a purpose that is more focused. What will you be explaining if it is an explanatory writing task? What information would you need to write an effective narrative? These are questions that you should be asking yourself.

4. Familiarize yourself with the Performance Task writing rubrics that are located in the appendix of this book. Highlight all of the key words that describe each score point. Be sure to look at all three genres because you could possibly have any of these types of writing tasks. If there is something that you do not understand, be sure to look up any parts of the rubric that confuse you. Take the

time to at least look at what constitutes a score of a "**4**." This will let you know what is expected of you in Part 2 of the Performance Task.

5. Take notes! Whether you choose to use the computer notetaking system or scratch paper, be sure to take notes on the information and content given. You will have more potential evidence and writing ideas if you take copious notes. This means include details from the text that could help you form an argument, help with an explanatory writing piece, or build a foundation for a narrative because Part 2 of the Performance Task will ask you to do one of those writing tasks. You will also be asked to cite textual evidence, so writing down details can help you with that. It is much easier to take the notes as you read than to keep returning to the sources, although it is permitted.

6. Use Part 1 of the Performance Task to help you with writing the argumentative essay, explanatory writing piece, or the narrative in Part 2. Part 1 will ask you to do some writing tasks that can help you think about the writing task in Part 2. For example, a question or item in Part 1 may ask you to support a statement with cited textual evidence from one or more of the sources. This could potentially help you in brainstorming ways to support a particular position that may help you if you needed to write an argumentative essay. Look at the items in Part 1, and think about how this could extend your ideas and beliefs.

7. Take the time to do some prewriting before you start Part 2 of the Performance Task. Effective prewriting activities are discussed in the next chapter. Select one of those, or use a favorite prewriting method if you already have one. Even if you only do prewriting for five minutes, you will potentially increase chances that your writing will be more focused and organized with more logic than if you just begin writing. Use your prewriting as you write.

8. After writing, be sure to read through your entire writing piece for Part 2 very carefully. Begin by revising. This means that you will add information or make changes to parts of your writing that are not clear or that do not make sense. Do this first before editing. You may consider adding more textual evidence to support your claims, or you may rework the plot structure of your narrative. These activities are part of the revision process. Once you are certain that your writing is clear, organized, and in-depth with content, then begin editing. Editing is when you look for spelling errors, incorrect punctuation, or capitalization issues. Be sure to read through your writing carefully.

9. Finally, reread the writing task directions one last time to ensure that you have answered all of the questions and that you have completed all of the tasks that

were asked of you. When your test is scored, evaluators will look to see that each part of the task is addressed in your writing piece. If anything is missing, return to your response to make any final additions that you deem necessary. Make sure that textual evidence is cited when it is asked of you. Always read your writing as many times as necessary in order to be sure that you covered everything.

PERFORMANCE TASK TESTING PRACTICE

Now you will work through a Performance Task in order to prepare for that portion of the test. Pay attention to the format and the prompts because they will be similar to the actual SBAC test that you will take. Follow as best as possible, and remember that you will not be able to go back to your Part 1 questions and answers once you go to Part 2, although you will have access to your notes from both parts. You may use scratch paper for your notes, or you may practice writing notes on a computer. Select what works best for you.

Physical Activity Performance Task

Issue: There is evidence that physical activity is a necessary part of a young person's life. Yet, are young people getting enough physical activity, and what can be done to encourage them to do that? Should schools get involved?

The issue of whether physical activity is truly necessary and whether schools should get involved is the focus of the school newspaper. The newspaper's editorial staff will read all of the entries from students and select a few to be featured on that page of the newspaper. You found the following three sources while researching that will aid your argument, and you intend to get it published in the newspaper.

Read all three of the sources provided. In ELA PT Part 1, you will be answering three questions based on the sources to help you think about the argument that you will make in your newspaper article. In ELA PT Part 2, you will be writing an argumentative newspaper article that defends a position that you are taking on this issue.

Directions: Read the following three sources. You may read all of the sources at any time during both parts of the Performance Task. Carefully read the information, and take notes as much as you need to in order to prepare for the argumentative news article that you will write in ELA PT Part 2.

Part One—Research Questions

You will answer three research questions in Part 1 of the Performance Task. Write your responses in the boxes provided. All three of these questions will be scored, so answer them thoughtfully. Address all parts of the question.

Part 1—Sources for Physical Activity Performance Task

Source #1

Information for "Physical Activity Facts" is from the following source:

https://www.cdc.gov/healthyschools/physicalactivity/facts.htm

Physical Activity Facts

- Regular physical activity in childhood and adolescence improves strength and endurance, helps build healthy bones and muscles, helps control weight, reduces anxiety and stress, increases self-esteem, and may improve blood pressure and cholesterol levels.
- The U.S. Department of Health and Human Services recommends that young people aged 6–17 years participate in at least 60 minutes of physical activity daily.
- In 2013, 27.1% of high school students surveyed had participated in at least 60 minutes per day of physical activity on all 7 days before the survey, and only 29% attended physical education class daily.
- Schools can promote physical activity through comprehensive school physical activity programs, including recess, classroom-based physical activity, intramural physical activity clubs, interscholastic sports, and physical education.
- Schools should ensure that physical education is provided to all students in all grades and is taught by qualified teachers.
- Schools can also work with community organizations to provide out-of-school-time physical activity programs and share physical activity facilities.

Physical Activity and the Health of Young People

Benefits of Regular Physical Activity

Regular physical activity—

- Helps build and maintain healthy bones and muscles.
- Helps reduce the risk of developing obesity and chronic diseases, such as diabetes, cardiovascular disease, and colon cancer.
- Reduces feelings of depression and anxiety and promotes psychological well-being.
- May help improve students' academic performance, including

  - Academic achievement and grades
  - Academic behavior, such as time on task
  - Factors that influence academic achievement, such as concentration and attentiveness in the classroom.

Long-Term Consequences of Physical Inactivity

- Overweight and obesity, which are influenced by physical inactivity and poor diet, can increase one's risk for diabetes, high blood pressure, high cholesterol, asthma, arthritis, and poor health status.
- Physical inactivity increases one's risk for dying prematurely, dying of heart disease, and developing diabetes, colon cancer, and high blood pressure.

Participation in Physical Activity by Young People

- In a nationally representative survey, 77% of children aged 9–13 years reported participating in free-time physical activity during the previous 7 days.
- In 2013, only 29% percent of high school students had participated in at least 60 minutes per day of physical activity on each of the 7 days before the survey.
- 15.2% percent of high school students had not participated in 60 or more minutes of any kind of physical activity on any day during the 7 days before the survey.
- Participation in physical activity declines as young people age.

Participation in Physical Education Classes

- In 2013, less than half (48%) of high school students (64% of 9th-grade students but only 35% of 12th-grade students) attended physical education classes in an average week.
- The percentage of high school students who attended physical education classes daily decreased from 42% in 1991 to 25% in 1995 and remained stable at that level until 2013 (29%).
- In 2013, 42% of 9th-grade students but only 20% of 12th-grade students attended physical education class daily.

Source #2

Information for "Physical Activity Guidelines" is from the following source:

https://www.cdc.gov/healthyschools/physicalactivity/guidelines.htm

Introduction

The Physical Activity Guidelines for Americans, issued by the U.S. Department of Health and Human Services, recommend that children and adolescents aged 6–17 years should have 60 minutes (1 hour) or more of physical activity each day.

Youth Physical Activity Guidelines

- Children and adolescents should have 60 minutes (1 hour) or more of physical activity daily.

  - **Aerobic:** Most of the 60 or more minutes a day should be either moderate- or vigorous-intensity aerobic physical activity and should include vigorous-intensity physical activity at least 3 days a week.
  - **Muscle-strengthening:** As part of their 60 or more minutes of daily physical activity, children and adolescents should include muscle-strengthening physical activity on at least 3 days of the week.
  - **Bone-strengthening:** As part of their 60 or more minutes of daily physical activity, children and adolescents should include bone-strengthening physical activity on at least 3 days of the week.

- It is important to encourage young people to participate in physical activities that are appropriate for their age, that are enjoyable, and that offer variety.

Source: U.S. Department of Health and Human Services. *Physical Activity Guidelines for Americans.* Washington, DC: U.S. Department of Health and Human Services, 2008.

Source #3

Information for "The Role of Schools" is from the following source:

https://www.cdc.gov/healthyschools/physicalactivity/guidelines.htm

The Role of Schools

Being physically active is one of the most important steps to being healthy. Schools are an ideal setting for teaching youth how to adopt and maintain a healthy, active lifestyle. Schools can help youth learn how to be physically active for a lifetime.

Why Should Schools Provide Physical Activity Programs?

- Youth who are physically active get physical and mental health benefits.
- Comprehensive school-based physical activity programs can help youth meet most of their physical activity needs.
- School-based physical activity programs benefit communities as well as students and schools.

How Does Physical Activity Help?

- Builds strong bones and muscles.
- Decreases the likelihood of developing obesity and risk factors for diseases like type 2 diabetes and heart disease.
- May reduce anxiety and depression and promote positive mental health.

How Much Physical Activity Do Youth Need?

- **Children and adolescents should do 60 minutes (1 hour) or more of physical activity daily.**

  - *Aerobic Activities:* Most of the 60 or more minutes per day should be either moderate- or vigorous-intensity aerobic physical activity. Vigorous-intensity physical activity should be included at least 3 days per week.

    - Examples of aerobic activities include bike riding, walking, running, dancing, and playing active games like tag, soccer, and basketball.

  - *Muscle-strengthening Activities:* Include muscle-strengthening physical activity on at least 3 days of the week as part of the 60 or more minutes.

    - Examples of muscle-strengthening activities for younger children include gymnastics, playing on a jungle gym, and climbing a tree.
    - Examples of muscle-strengthening activities for adolescents include push-ups, pull-ups, and weightlifting exercises.

  - *Bone-strengthening Activities:* Include bone-strengthening physical activity on at least 3 days of the week as part of the 60 or more minutes.

    - Examples of bone-strengthening activities include hopping, skipping, jumping, running, and sports like gymnastics, basketball, and tennis.

- Some activities may address more than one category at a time. For example, gymnastics is both muscle-strengthening and bone-strengthening while running is aerobic and bone-strengthening.
- Activities should be age-appropriate, enjoyable, and offer variety.

How Physically Active Are Youth?

- In 2007, only 17% of 9th–12th grade students said they were physically active at least 60 minutes per day.
- Among 9–13 year olds, only 39% said they participated in organized physical activity.
- In 2007, only 30% of 9th–12th grade students said they attended physical education classes every day.
- In 1969, 41% of students walked or biked to school; by 2001, only 13% of students walked or biked to school.

How Does Physical Activity Affect Academic Achievement?

- Physical activity can help youth improve their concentration, memory, and classroom behavior.
- Youth who spend more time in physical education class do not have lower test scores than youths who spend less time in physical education class.
- Elementary school girls who participated in more physical education had better math and reading tests scores than girls who had less time in physical education.

What Can Schools Do To Promote Physical Activity for Youth?

- Have policies that provide time for organized physical activity and free play.
- Provide information to parents about the benefits of physical activity in messages sent home and at school events.
- Encourage staff to be active. School staff and school leadership are role models for students.
- Encourage families and local groups to be involved in school-based physical activities and events.

1. Look at the sources and determine **three** reasons why young people should follow the guidelines for physical activity. Cite textual evidence from **two** of the sources.

2. What evidence can you find that would support the claim that schools have a role in this issue? Find textual evidence from at least **two** sources that would support this claim.

3. Some of the sources about how physically active young people are have differing factual information. Based on the information from all **three** sources, describe what this tells you about physical activity in young people including the benefits and consequences that exist.

(Answers are on pages 152–153.)

Part Two—Writing

Directions: You will have access to all three sources and your notes as you plan, draft, revise, and edit your newspaper article. Read the following information carefully before beginning the writing process.

Your Assignment: You are working on a newspaper article that you would like featured in the school newspaper. You will need to take a position on whether physical activity should increase for most young people and on whether schools should take a role in the issue. You will need to provide evidence from the sources to support your argument and to create counterarguments for varying perspectives.

Argumentative Writing Scoring

Your argumentative writing piece will be scored on the following categories:

1. **Organization/Purpose**—Is there a clear and effective organizational structure? Is there a sense of unity in the writing? Is there an introduction? Are there transitions between ideas? Is there a conclusion? Are ideas logically placed? Are opposing viewpoints anticipated and addressed?

2. **Evidence/Elaboration**—Is there convincing elaboration of evidence that is used to support claims and arguments? Are the arguments reasonable? Are ideas developed? Is there comprehensive evidence? Are citations clearly marked? Is vocabulary appropriate for the purpose and audience? Is the style effective and appropriate?

3. **Conventions**—Does the response have a sufficient command of conventions including sentence structure, punctuation, capitalization, grammar, and spelling?

Work on your argumentative newspaper article. Be sure to manage time, so that you can plan, write, revise, and edit your argumentative article.

You will have access to word-processing tools and spell check.

Final instructions: In this part, you will be expected to write a multi-paragraph essay. Write as much as you can, and be comprehensive. Write your response in the following box which will expand as you type. Refer to your notes and the sources whenever you need to in order to complete this task.

Argumentative Writing Task Continued:

(Answers are on pages 153–155.)

Writing

CHAPTER 5

Understanding All Writing Sections of the SBAC

There is writing throughout all of the sections of the SBAC test. They will be interspersed throughout the test. This means that you will be asked to write as you move through the Computer-Adaptive Test (CAT) for the selected-response and constructed-response and as you take the Performance Task (PT). Remember that the selected-response and constructed-response are mingled together, so although you may answer the selected-response with a letter, the following item or question could be a constructed-response-type item. They are mixed together. The Performance Task is a separate part of the test, so you will only have constructed-response and a lengthy writing task in both parts of the Performance Task.

Remember that you will want to strategize differently for the various parts of writing tasks required of you as the scoring may differ from one another. For example, a constructed-response in the CAT or PT will require that you answer more briefly, but you need to address all parts of the item or question. Otherwise, your score could be graded significantly lower. Always be mindful of addressing all parts of the question. Most of these responses are not scored for conventions (grammar, punctuation, and spelling) although you will want to use your best skills to avoid confusing the reader. This could interfere with the reading and result in a lower score than if you were more careful with your mechanics. The first rule of thumb for the constructed-response is to answer all parts of the item or question. If the item asks you to do three things, do all of the three things. If the item asks you to cite two sources, cite two sources. This will ensure that you receive all of the points that you can possibly earn.

In the constructed-response sections, aim to be crystal clear about what you are trying to say. Reread your response multiple times to make sure that you are saying what you mean. Sometimes when you are writing your first draft, you may not notice how you digressed or didn't stay focused on the topic. Be sure that your response says what you mean and is clearly articulated, so that the reader understands the message you are trying to communicate. Once you are happy with the response, read it one last time to comb through it and see if minor revisions or edits are necessary. Remember revisions include adding or reorganizing ideas, and edits are checking for conventions and mechanics.

Finally, be concise, but thorough. This is a challenging thing to do. When you are concise, you are using less words that are effectively communicating the message. When you are thorough, you are being detailed and comprehensive. This is a hard thing to do, but it will strengthen your writing and help you maximize on time. Good writers are always trying to be clear with the least amount of words as possible. This does not mean that you should make your answer shorter but more shallow. Your answer must have depth. Just practice writing a sentence, and then try to say it in as few words as possible. You will improve on this skill the more you practice it. A word of caution, though… you need to be detailed. If you sacrifice detail, then it will not be worth it to be concise. You need the content. You just want to say it in as few words as possible. This takes practice! Try this strategy as you practice writing in this book.

The Performance Task has two parts. In Part 1, you will have constructed-response items or questions. These are similar to the constructed-response items on the CAT. However, there is one major thing to think about. This section of the Performance Task will be very specific about how many sources to provide in your textual evidence. Pay close attention to these numbers. If the question asks you to give three reasons, ensure that you are providing three reasons. If the item asks you to cite two sources, cite two sources. This is where the points are gathered… when you are careful to include everything asked of you! This is probably the most critical thing to think about in ELA PT Part 1 of the Performance Task. Again, you will not be scored on conventions; however, make sure that you are using mechanics as precisely as possible. You run the risk of confusing your reader and scorer should there be many convention errors. Remember that conventions include grammar, punctuation, capitalization, and spelling.

Yet another way of strategizing occurs as you tackle ELA PT Part 2 of the Performance Task. This is a multi-paragraph response, so it is essential that you get in the habit of doing some prewriting. The following section will give you some ideas for prewriting for both the constructed-response items and for both parts of the Performance Task test. It is strongly recommended that you do some type of prewriting. Even five minutes can help you immensely when writing your essay or narrative because it will organize your thoughts and put content on paper. It will allow you to see your main points clearly, and it will inform you on what to include. Another strategy is to revise and to edit, which is also covered in the following sections. This can ensure that you include the content necessary to provide adequate coverage of the topic, and it will make certain that you are understood if you have few convention errors. Follow the suggestions in this chapter, and you will see improvement in your writing for sure.

Finally, understand that both the constructed-response items and Performance Task items are on-demand writing tasks. This means that you are asked to write quickly within a reasonable timeline. Your responses do not have to be perfect because they will not be scrutinized as if you had a week to write them. Still conform to the strategies in this chapter, but take a deep breath. Perfection is not expected. Do the best that you can with the time and skills that you have. Do the prewriting, drafting, revising, and editing, but be assured that you will do well if you use all of the strategies in this book!

Effective Prewriting Activities

Prewriting is a critical part of the writing process that you should not skip for any of the written parts of the SBAC test! There are different prewriting strategies for different parts of the test, but you should always spend at least two minutes for constructed-response items and at least 5–10 minutes for the longer written responses which are in ELA PT Part 2 of the Performance Task test. This chapter will break down some of the prewriting activities and strategies for each type of written response. When you get to the longer written responses, pay attention to the various types of prewriting ideas in this section, and select what works best for you. Everyone has a different learning and writing style which affects how useful the various prewriting activities can be for each person.

For the constructed-response items or questions, you want to spend about two minutes putting together your ideas. The main strategy here is organizing your ideas and making sure that all of the necessary content is included. Generally, your constructed-response items will be preceded by a passage or multiple sources such as in ELA PT Part 1 of the Performance Task. You may choose to use the computer to take notes, or you may elect to use paper and pencil. Use whatever makes you the most comfortable. If using the computer really helps you, use that. If you need to see it on paper, ask for scratch paper as that is permitted during the test.

In your prewriting for the constructed-response, it may help to quickly jot down the things asked of you, so that you can be sure to answer the question. For example, let's look at an item from the previous chapter in ELA PT Part 1 of the Performance Task.

1. Look at all three sources and determine three reasons why young people should follow the guidelines for physical activity. Cite textual evidence from two of the sources.

   This question gives you all of the instructions that you need to respond to the item successfully. Your prewriting strategy here will be to make sure that all parts are addressed. Look at the sample prewriting activity below.

Prewriting Activity:

Three Reasons Why Young People Should Do Physical Activity:

   1.

   2.

   3.

Textual Evidence:

   Source #1:

   Source #2:

When you quickly jot this skeleton down, it increases your chances of addressing all parts of the constructed-response item or question. You will see that you need three reasons which you can fill in as you reread the sources. You also have two spaces allotted for two sources which will remind you that you need to include two different sources. This takes you two to three minutes to do, but can significantly increase your chances of addressing all of the parts of the writing task. It is best to do this consistently and frequently whenever you see a constructed-response item. It really takes little time and will help focus your reading and allow you to organize your ideas better.

Prewriting for ELA PT Part 2 of the Performance Task is a little more complicated because you have to plan, draft, revise, and edit a multi-paragraph written response. This means that you will have to look at a few ideas that may help you with organizing your thoughts and with including the content necessary to earn a high score. In this section, look at all of the choices. If you have a favorite prewriting activity that works for you, then use it. There will be a few ideas here to get you started. Try to prewrite for approximately 7–10 minutes for this writing task because it is longer. This is a good rule of thumb. If you take a little less time or a little more time, that should be fine. Just try to spend no less than five minutes and no more than fifteen minutes to do the prewriting activity for this writing task. Let's look at ELA PT Part 2 of the Performance Task in the previous chapter.

Performance Task—Part Two

Your Assignment: You are working on a newspaper article that you would like featured in the school newspaper. You will need to take a position on whether physical activity should increase for most young people and on whether schools should take a role on the issue. You will need to provide evidence from the sources to support your argument and to create counterarguments for varying perspectives.

Refer back to this assignment as you look at the two prewriting activities that are illustrated in this section. You may do a simple listing with some labeling similar to the constructed-response prewriting example. You may even opt to do the cluster diagramming that can help you in a visual way as well. Different people find different prewriting activities more useful, so do not be afraid to try both activities or use one of your own ideas!

The first prewriting activity is a mix of listing, outlining, and labeling. The labeling ensures that you cover all of the parts of the writing task. It is close to an outline, but you will spend time listing the points and examples. Using this hybrid of prewriting strategies will make sure that you have a clear position, that you will have a focused introduction and conclusion, and that you will have examples and counterarguments that support your claims and assertions. Just list your ideas, and they will turn your written response into an organized article with adequate support and counterarguments to strengthen the argument. The goal is to narrow down your ideas into a focused, intentional, and organized writing piece. This will increase the likelihood that you cover all parts of the writing task.

Prewriting Activity: Listing with Labeling

Performance Task—Part Two: Argumentative Newspaper Article

Position (*On increasing physical activity and the role of the school*):

My position is:

Introduction:

- Point One—

- Point Two—

- Point Three (*Counterarguments*)—

Paragraph One:

- Point One—

- Examples—

Paragraph Two:

- Point Two—

- Examples—

Paragraph Three:

- Counterarguments—

Conclusion:

- Point One—

- Point Two—

- Point Three—

The second prewriting activity is a version of cluster diagramming. This gives the writer a visual way of looking at ideas, and helps organize the content. This type of prewriting activity has a brainstorming component because you organize your ideas after doing a little bit of brainstorming. This helps if you are unclear about all of your ideas. It allows you to focus on the important parts.

Prewriting Activity: Cluster Diagramming

Performance Task—Part Two: Argumentative Newspaper Article

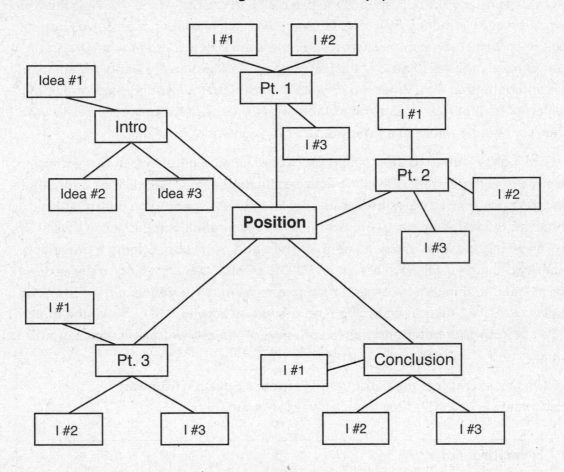

The second prewriting activity above can accommodate even more ideas. The "I's" stand for ideas, and the "Pt.'s" represent points. You can even number the idea boxes in the end, so you know which order to put the ideas in for each paragraph. Notice how you can organize your ideas while just getting them out on paper. This prewriting activity would probably not work with a computer notepad, so you would need paper-based notetaking for this prewriting method. Try out both, and see which works best for you. You may even use both, but in different writing scenarios. For example, you may use the first prewriting activity for argumentative essays, but you may use a version of the second prewriting activity to write a narrative. Get comfortable with a variety of methods, so that you can select the one that works best for you with a given writing task.

Linking Prewriting to the Drafting Process

As stated previously, it will be important that you have a number of prewriting activities under your belt, so that you can pick and choose which one best fits your situation at a moment's notice. Some prewriting activities lend themselves better to the constructed-response items, and others are better for the multi-paragraph assignment in ELA PT Part 2 of the Performance Task. Some are better for specific writing genres as well. What works well for an explanatory writing piece may be different for a narrative. Get comfortable with as many prewriting activities as you can, so that you will have a variety of tools in your writing tool belt.

Linking prewriting to the drafting process will look different in various writing tasks and with different prewriting activities. In this section, we will look at the three examples of prewriting in the last section. You should spend time thinking about how this works for whatever prewriting activity you select, but this section will give you a good idea of how to do that. The good news about doing a prewriting activity is that you will have almost an outline of what you are going to say, so you don't need to think about organizing thoughts as much as you would if you wrote the constructed-response cold from no prewriting activity. You can take the ideas straight from your notes and form a cohesive, organized written response more quickly and efficiently.

The first example is the constructed-response question from Part 1 of the Performance Task. The prewriting activity looks like this:

Prewriting Activity:

Three Reasons Why Young People Should Do Physical Activity:

1.

2.

3.

Textual Evidence:

Source #1:

Source #2:

This prewriting activity, when filled in, enables the writer to make sure that all bases are covered. The only real decisions that need to be made here are choosing which textual evidence to use to support one or more of the three reasons. After that, a simple drafting of what textual evidence is paired with what reason can quickly happen. Here is a skeleton of what you may write for this constructed-response question:

Possible Constructed-Response Answer

Three reasons why young people should do physical activity are...

Source #1 supports reason one in that...

Source #1 also supports reason two in that...

Source #2 supports reason three because...

Because you did the prewriting activity, you are certain that you have addressed all of the parts of the constructed-response item.

Look at the first prewriting activity for ELA PT Part 2 of the Performance Task that is included in the previous section of this chapter. This is the listing with labeling prewriting activity. Linking this prewriting to drafting is fairly simple as well. Form your introductory paragraph by writing your position and three points. You will add more writing than the list, but your ideas are there. In your first support paragraph, write your point with examples from the text. Keep going until you reach the conclusion. Then restate your position and your three points. Again, the ideas are already there because you did the prewriting activity. You will need to add textual evidence to support each point, so hopefully those are located in the notes that you took as you read the available sources.

The second prewriting activity for ELA PT Part 2 of the Performance Task is a cluster diagram. This is similar to the process in the first prewriting activity. The main difference is that you will be pulling ideas and points from a more visual representation of your argumentative newspaper article. This may take you a little longer as you translate the ideas and points into words and sentences for your multi-paragraph writing task. Note that some students do very well with this type of prewriting. Determine which one suits you the best, and go for it! Linking the prewriting activity to drafting a written response may be easier for you when using listing and labeling. Maybe you will use that for a written task such as this one. You will be making these decisions.

Using Evidence and Research

You will be expected to use your research skills in order to find textual evidence that supports your claims and assertions. This is a very important part of the writing process. As you read text and sources, you need to take notes whether that be on the computer or on scratch paper. Finding evidence as soon as possible buys you more time to spend your energy on the planning and drafting part of the writing process. It is good to plan your essay first and determine what points you are going to make before selecting the actual textual evidence that you will use to support those points. This doesn't mean that you should skip taking notes on important parts of the passage as you read it for the first time. The notes will help clue you in on what is significant in the text which will, in turn, tell you what points to make. It is probable then that you will use your notes to support those points. It is a cyclical process. Follow this process, and you should do well with finding textual evidence that supports your main points.

Another tip for finding evidence is to highlight important parts of the passages and text. This can also help you pinpoint the best support for your written responses. Remember that for the research aspect of the writing process, you are being assessed on how well you can use a critical eye when reading the various sources given. Practice analyzing and evaluating the text and passages that you read as much as possible. For example, read to see what the underlying meanings are, and evaluate how effective the arguments are. You are not just reading for content when you are using research skills. Instead, you are critically thinking about what the author is trying to communicate to you along with determining if the author was successful in doing this.

Revising and Editing on the Fly

When you revise, you are looking for specific things in your written responses. You are definitely looking to see that your central ideas and details are focused. Are they effective and efficient? If not, you will want to revise and make changes or additions. Revision occurs after you are done drafting your written response. Always spend some time on revising. Writers rarely get it all on the first draft. Check to make sure that you addressed all parts of the item or question. Make sure that your textual evidence best supports your main points. Determine if you go off on tangents—that means to figure out if you stray from the main topics. All of this can be done in just a short amount of time, so it is worth it to spend the extra minutes on this. Ensure that all of your points, textual evidence, and explanations make sense. Sometimes writers will write quickly and not realize that something is unclear. Check for all of these things when revising.

Editing will be the final part of the writing process. You have planned what you are going to say in the prewriting stage; you have drafted a written response; you revised your work and made appropriate changes and additions; and now you are ready to edit your work. Editing simply means scanning your writing for convention errors (grammar, spelling, punctuation, and capitalization). If convention errors interfere with the reading of your written responses, then scorers may be forced to give you a lower score. A simple review of your final response will help you avoid this situation. Check for conventions for every written response. Again, it takes very little time, and it can result in a better score just because you took the extra minutes to check your work.

ELA Practice Test

Computer-Adaptive Test

Now it is your turn to take an SBAC ELA Practice Test from start to finish. The selected-response and constructed-response items or questions will be intermingled throughout this practice test because that is what you will see on the actual SBAC test administered in the spring months. It is recommended that you try to complete the selected-response and constructed-response items or questions from the first part of this test in one sitting. Then on another day, complete the two parts of the Performance Task. You will find all of the possible answers to each part of this test in chapter seven. You may write in this book, or you may opt to type your answers on a computer. This is up to you. Just realize that you will be typing your responses on the actual test, so you may want to practice composing written responses on your computer. Good luck!

Selected-Response and Constructed-Response Tasks

Directions: Read the text. Then answer questions 1-9.

Heidi
by Johanna Spyri

Chapter I. Up the Mountain to Alm-Uncle

From the old and pleasantly situated village of Mayenfeld, a footpath winds through green and shady meadows to the foot of the mountains, which on this side look down from their stern and lofty heights upon the valley below. The land grows gradually wilder as the path ascends, and the climber has not gone far before he begins to inhale the fragrance of the short grass and sturdy mountain-plants, for the way is steep and leads directly up to the summits above.

On a clear sunny morning in June two figures might be seen climbing the narrow mountain path; one, a tall strong-looking girl, the other a child whom she was leading by the hand, and whose little cheeks were so aglow with heat that the crimson color could be seen even through the dark, sunburnt skin. And this was hardly to be wondered at, for in spite of the hot June sun the child was clothed as if to keep off the bitterest frost. She did not look more than five years old, if as much, but what her natural figure was like, it would have been hard to say, for she had apparently two, if not three dresses, one above the other, and over these a thick red woollen shawl wound round about her, so that the little body presented a shapeless appearance, as, with its small feet shod in thick, nailed mountain-shoes, it slowly and laboriously plodded its way up in the heat. The two must have left the valley a good hour's walk behind them, when they came to the hamlet known as Dorfli, which is situated half-way up the mountain. Here the wayfarers met with greetings from all sides, some calling to them from windows, some from open doors, others from outside, for the elder girl was now in her old home. She did not, however, pause in her walk to respond to her friends' welcoming cries and questions, but passed on without stopping for a moment until she reached the last of the scattered houses of the hamlet. Here a voice called to her from the door: "Wait a moment, Dete; if you are going up higher, I will come with you."

The girl thus addressed stood still, and the child immediately let go her hand and seated herself on the ground.

"Are you tired, Heidi?" asked her companion.

"No, I am hot," answered the child.

"We shall soon get to the top now. You must walk bravely on a little longer, and take good long steps, and in another hour we shall be there," said Dete in an encouraging voice.

They were now joined by a stout, good-natured-looking woman, who walked on ahead with her old acquaintance, the two breaking forth at once into lively conversation about everybody and everything in Dorfli and its surroundings, while the child wandered behind them.

"And where are you off to with the child?" asked the one who had just joined the party. "I suppose it is the child your sister left?"

"Yes," answered Dete. "I am taking her up to Uncle, where she must stay."

"The child stay up there with Alm-Uncle! You must be out of your senses, Dete! How can you think of such a thing! The old man, however, will soon send you and your proposal packing off home again!"

"He cannot very well do that, seeing that he is her grandfather. He must do something for her. I have had the charge of the child till now, and I can tell you, Barbel, I am not going to give up the chance which has just fallen to me of getting a good place, for her sake. It is for the grandfather now to do his duty by her."

"That would be all very well if he were like other people," asseverated stout Barbel warmly, "but you know what he is. And what can he do with a child, especially with one so young! The child cannot possibly live with him. But where are you thinking of going yourself?"

"To Frankfurt, where an extra good place awaits me," answered Dete. "The people I am going to were down at the Baths last summer, and it was part of my duty to attend upon their rooms. They would have liked then to take me away with them, but I could not leave. Now they are there again and have repeated their offer, and I intend to go with them, you may make up your mind to that!"

"I am glad I am not the child!" exclaimed Barbel, with a gesture of horrified pity. "Not a creature knows anything about the old man up there! He will have nothing to do with anybody, and never sets his foot inside a church from one year's end to another. When he does come down once in a while, everybody clears out of the way of him and his big stick. The mere sight of him, with his bushy grey eyebrows and his immense beard, is alarming enough. He looks like any old heathen or Indian, and few would care to meet him alone."

"Well, and what of that?" said Dete, in a defiant voice, "he is the grandfather all the same, and must look after the child. He is not likely to do her any harm, and if he does, he will be answerable for it, not I."

"I should very much like to know," continued Barbel, in an inquiring tone of voice, "what the old man has on his conscience that he looks as he does, and lives up there on the mountain like a hermit, hardly ever allowing himself to be seen. All kinds of things are said about him. You, Dete, however, must certainly have learnt a good deal concerning him from your sister—am I not right?"

"You are right, I did, but I am not going to repeat what I heard; if it should come to his ears I should get into trouble about it."

Now Barbel had for long past been most anxious to ascertain particulars about Alm-Uncle, as she could not understand why he seemed to feel such hatred towards his fellow-creatures, and insisted on living all alone, or why people spoke about him half in whispers, as if afraid to say anything against him, and yet unwilling to take his Part. Moreover, Barbel was in ignorance as to why all the people in Dorfli called him Alm-Uncle, for he could not possibly be uncle to everybody living there. As, however, it was the custom, she did like the rest and called the old man Uncle. Barbel had only lived in Dorfli since her marriage, which had taken place not long before. Previous to that her home had been below in Prattigau, so that she was not well acquainted with all the events that had ever taken place, and with all the people who had ever lived in Dorfli and its neighborhood. Dete, on the contrary, had been born in Dorfli, and had lived there with her mother until the death of the latter the year before, and had then gone over to the Baths at Ragatz and taken service in the large hotel there as chambermaid. On the morning of this day she had come all the way from Ragatz with the child, a friend having given them a lift in a hay-cart as far as Mayenfeld. Barbel was therefore determined not to lose this good opportunity of satisfying her curiosity. She put her arm through Dete's in a confidential sort of way, and said: "I know I can find out the real truth from you, and the meaning of all these tales that are afloat about him. I believe you know the whole story. Now do just tell me what is wrong with the old man, and if he was always shunned as he is now, and was always such a misanthrope."

1. Read the following sentence from the text.

From the old and pleasantly situated village of Mayenfeld, a footpath winds through green and shady meadows to the foot of the mountains, which on this side look down from their stern and **lofty** heights upon the valley below.

Using context clues, determine the possible meaning(s) of "lofty."
Select **two** definitions that apply.

☐ A. Lofty means elevated at a higher level.
☐ B. Lofty means being stern.
☐ C. Lofty means old and pleasant.
☐ D. Lofty means rich and thick.
☐ E. Lofty means of a great height.
☐ F. Lofty means resilient.

2. Read the following paragraph from the passage.

From the old and pleasantly situated village of Mayenfeld, a footpath winds through green and shady meadows to the foot of the mountains, which on this side look down from their stern and lofty heights upon the valley below. The land grows gradually wilder as the path ascends, and the climber has not gone far before he begins to inhale the fragrance of the short grass and sturdy mountain-plants, for the way is steep and leads directly up to the summits above.

The first paragraph introduces the setting of the story in terms of the place where the story occurs. Why do you think the author uses words such as "stern" and "sturdy" to describe the structures of the land? Select **three** responses that apply.

- ☐ A. The author wants the reader to understand how beautiful the environment is in the story.
- ☐ B. The author wants to set the tone of the story.
- ☐ C. The author wants to communicate how dangerous the surroundings are.
- ☐ D. The author wants the reader to pay attention to the environment.
- ☐ E. The stern and sturdy land describes a stern and sturdy tone.
- ☐ F. The words stern and sturdy focus the reader on the strength of the land.
- ☐ G. The environs are stern and sturdy like the characters.

3. How does the introduction of characters in the second paragraph build the reader's interest in the story? What part of the plot structure does it support? Select **all** that apply.

- ☐ A. The introduction each character builds reader interest by describing the characters in detail.
- ☐ B. The rising action of the plot structure is introduced.
- ☐ C. The introduction of each character builds reader interest as it talks about the grueling trip.
- ☐ D. The climax of the plot structure is introduced.
- ☐ E. The introduction of each character builds reader interest as it describes an unusual situation in how the child is dressed.
- ☐ F. The exposition of the plot structure is introduced.
- ☐ G. The introduction of the characters builds reader interest by including some dialogue.

4. Read the following paragraph from the text.

She did not look more than five years old, if as much, but what her natural figure was like, it would have been hard to say, for she had apparently two, if not three dresses, one above the other, and over these a thick red woollen shawl wound round about her, so that the little body presented a shapeless appearance, as, with its small feet shod in thick, nailed mountain-shoes, it slowly and **laboriously plodded** its way up in the heat.

Part A

Highlight the context clues that help define what "laboriously plodded" means.

Part B

Define what "laboriously plodded" means based on the context clues that you identified in Part A.

- ○ A. The young girl was dressed with a lot of clothes, so "laboriously plodded" must mean being hot and heavy from exertion.
- ○ B. The young girl was dressed heavily, so "laboriously plodded" must mean working hard at walking like dragging her feet with a lot of weight.
- ○ C. The young girl was inappropriately clothed, so "laboriously plodded" must mean that she was tired and hungry.
- ○ D. The young girl was wearing three dresses, so "laboriously plodded" must mean that she was ready to rest.

5. What does the exchange of dialogue between Dete and Barbel reveal about Alm-Uncle? How does this affect the plot structure? Cite textual evidence to support your claims.

Paraphrasing the main points or events.	
Interpreting the text.	
Evidence-based response provided.	
Explanatory response provided.	

Write your constructed-response in the box below.

6. What point of view is used in this passage? How does this affect the character development?

Evidence-based response provided.	
Explanatory response provided.	

Write your constructed-response in the box below.

7. How does the author contrast the points of view of Dete and Barbel in this passage? What does this tell the reader about each character? How does it affect the plot structure?

Evidence-based response provided.	
Explanatory response provided.	

Write your constructed-response in the box below.

8. Based on the dialogue of other characters, how does the author characterize Alm-Uncle? Cite textual evidence to support your assertions.

Evidence-based response provided.	
Explanatory response provided.	

Write your constructed-response in the box below.

9. What is a possible theme of this reading passage?

Evidence-based response provided.	
Explanatory response provided.	

Write your constructed-response in the box below.

Directions: Read the text. Then answer questions 10–18.

Patrick Henry's Speech to the Virginia House of Burgesses, Richmond, Virginia
March 23, 1775
by Patrick Henry

Source: *William Wirt, The Life and Character of Patrick Henry (1817)*

No man thinks more highly than I do of the patriotism, as well as abilities, of the very worthy gentlemen who have just addressed the House. But different men often see the same subject in different lights; and, therefore, I hope that it will not be thought disrespectful to those gentlemen, if, entertaining as I do opinions of a character very opposite to theirs, I shall speak forth my sentiments freely and without reserve.

This is no time for ceremony. The question before the House is one of awful moment to this country. For my own part I consider it as nothing less than a question of freedom or slavery; and in proportion to the magnitude of the subject ought to be the freedom of the debate. It is only in this way that we can hope to arrive at truth, and fulfill the great responsibility which we hold to God and our country. Should I keep back my opinions at such a time, through fear of giving offense, I should consider myself as guilty of treason towards my country, and of an act of disloyalty towards the majesty of heaven, which I revere above all earthly kings.

Mr. President, it is natural to man to indulge in the illusions of hope. We are apt to shut our eyes against a painful truth, and listen to the song of that siren, till she transforms us into beasts. Is this the part of wise men, engaged in a great and arduous struggle for liberty? Are we disposed to be of the number of those who, having eyes, see not, and having ears, hear not, the things which so nearly concern their temporal salvation?

For my part, whatever anguish of spirit it may cost, I am willing to know the whole truth—to know the worst and to provide for it. I have but one lamp by which my feet are guided; and that is the lamp of experience. I know of no way of judging of the future but by the past. And judging by the past, I wish to know what there has been in the conduct of the British ministry for the last ten years, to justify those hopes with which gentlemen have been pleased to solace themselves and the House?

Is it that insidious smile with which our petition has been lately received? Trust it not, sir; it will prove a snare to your feet. Suffer not yourselves to be betrayed with a kiss. Ask yourselves how this gracious reception of our petition comports with these warlike preparations which cover our waters and darken our land. Are fleets and armies necessary to a work of love and reconciliation? Have we shown ourselves so unwilling to be reconciled that force must be called in to win back our love? Let us not deceive ourselves, sir. These are the implements of war and subjugation—the last arguments to which kings resort. I ask gentlemen, sir, what means this martial array, if its purpose be not to force us to submission? Can gentlemen assign any other possible motives for it? Has Great Britain any enemy, in this quarter of the world, to call for all this accumulation of navies and armies?

No, sir, she has none. They are meant for us; they can be meant for no other. They are sent over to bind and rivet upon us those chains which the British ministry have been so long forging. And what have we to oppose to them? Shall we try argument? Sir, we have been trying that for the last ten years. Have we anything new to offer on the subject? Nothing.

We have held the subject up in every light of which it is capable; but it has been all in vain. Shall we resort to entreaty and humble supplication? What terms shall we find which have not been already exhausted? Let us not, I beseech you, sir, deceive ourselves longer.

Sir, we have done everything that could be done to avert the storm which is now coming on. We have petitioned; we have remonstrated; we have supplicated; we have prostrated ourselves before the throne, and have implored its interposition to arrest the tyrannical hands of the ministry and Parliament.

Our petitions have been slighted; our remonstrances have produced additional violence and insult; our supplications have been disregarded; and we have been spurned, with contempt, from the foot of the throne. In vain, after these things, may we indulge the fond hope of peace and reconciliation. There is no longer any room for hope.

If we wish to be free—if we mean to preserve inviolate those inestimable privileges for which we have been so long contending—if we mean not basely to abandon the noble struggle in which we have been so long engaged, and which we have pledged ourselves never to abandon until the glorious object of our contest shall be obtained, we must fight! I repeat it, sir, we must fight! An appeal to arms and to the God of Hosts is all that is left us!

They tell us, sir, that we are weak—unable to cope with so formidable an adversary. But when shall we be stronger? Will it be the next week, or the next year? Will it be when we are totally disarmed, and when a British guard shall be stationed in every house? Shall we gather strength by irresolution and inaction? Shall we acquire the means of effectual resistance, by lying supinely on our backs, and hugging the delusive phantom of hope, until our enemies shall have bound us hand and foot?

Sir, we are not weak, if we make a proper use of the means which the God of nature hath placed in our power. Three millions of people, armed in the holy cause of liberty, and in such a country as that which we possess, are invincible by any force which our enemy can send against us. Besides, sir, we shall not fight our battles alone. There is a just God who presides over the destinies of nations, and who will raise up friends to fight our battles for us.

The battle, sir, is not to the strong alone; it is to the vigilant, the active, the brave. Besides, sir, we have no election. If we were base enough to desire it, it is now too late to retire from the contest. There is no retreat but in submission and slavery! Our chains are forged! Their clanking may be heard on the plains of Boston! The war is inevitable—and let it come! I repeat it, sir, let it come!

It is in vain, sir, to extenuate the matter. Gentlemen may cry, "Peace! Peace!"—but there is no peace. The war is actually begun! The next gale that sweeps from the north will bring to our ears the clash of resounding arms! Our brethren are already in the field! Why stand we here idle? What is it that gentlemen wish? What would they have? Is life so dear, or peace so sweet, as to be purchased at the price of chains and slavery? Forbid it, Almighty God! I know not what course others may take; but as for me, give me liberty, or give me death!

Patrick Henry – March 23, 1775

10. Read the following first paragraph of Henry's speech.

No man thinks more highly than I do of the patriotism, as well as abilities, of the very worthy gentlemen who have just addressed the House. But different men often see the same subject in different lights; and, therefore, I hope that it will not be thought disrespectful to those gentlemen, if, entertaining as I do opinions of a character very opposite to theirs, I shall speak forth my sentiments freely and without reserve.

What main purpose does this introduction have for the rest of Henry's argument? Select **two** responses that **best** apply.

☐ A. Henry is ensuring that he does not offend his fellow brethren in the House.

☐ B. Henry is focusing his argument through this introduction.

☐ C. Henry is setting up his argument by first commending his adversaries to prepare them for his argument.

☐ D. Henry is apologetic about his need for speaking about the subject of fighting for liberty.

☐ E. Henry is tracing his argument before explaining the details.

☐ F. Henry is evaluating the arguments of his fellow colleagues.

☐ G. Henry is being humble and apologetic.

11. Look at the following sentence from the second paragraph.

I consider it as nothing less than a question of freedom or slavery.

What does this sentence represent? Select **two** statements that apply.

☐ A. This sentence is a claim, or position, that Henry is stating.

☐ B. This is a counterargument that Henry is making.

☐ C. This is an example of evidence to support Henry's point.

☐ D. This is an argument that Henry is setting up for his speech.

☐ E. This is an example of figurative language.

☐ F. This is an evaluation of his opponent's arguments.

12. What purpose does Henry fulfill in the entire second paragraph? Select **three** responses that **best** apply.

☐ A. Henry wants to be sure that he does not offend his fellow colleagues.
☐ B. Henry makes the argument that he will not commit treason.
☐ C. Henry reassures the House that disloyalty will not be an issue.
☐ D. Henry establishes the need for dialogue in order to find truth.
☐ E. Henry states the gravity of the topic.
☐ F. Henry relinquishes his argument.
☐ G. Henry appeals to the emotions of his opponents.

13. What does Henry mean when he says that "it is natural to man to indulge in the illusions of hope?" Select **three** responses that **best** apply.

☐ A. Henry is commenting that it is natural for men to want to give in to comrades.
☐ B. Henry is calling "illusions of hope" a positive way to deal with the problem.
☐ C. Henry is stating that it is easy for men to hope for the best, which deludes and does not resolve the problem.
☐ D. Henry is referring to hope as the best way to perceive the situation in this country.
☐ E. Henry is emphasizing that hope will not help in this situation.
☐ F. Henry cautions his brethren about false hope.

14. Look at the following statement.

They are sent over to bind and rivet upon us those chains which the British ministry have been so long forging.

What is the figurative meaning of this comment?

- ○ A. Henry talks about how the British are moving the situation forward.
- ○ B. Henry uses the image of "chains" to explain how England has imprisoned this country.
- ○ C. Henry states that the British are binding ties of connection with this new country.
- ○ D. Henry claims that the British are having trouble controlling this extension of England.

15. What does Henry mean by "the storm which is now coming on?" Select **two** responses that **best** apply.

- ☐ A. The storm is a metaphor for the war that is ahead.
- ☐ B. Henry is describing the problems through a simile.
- ☐ C. Henry is making a thematic thread that will run through the speech.
- ☐ D. Henry is using the storm as a symbol of the turmoil and fighting that is imminent.
- ☐ E. Henry is using a hyperbole to emphasize his point.
- ☐ F. Henry is using figurative language to make an effective point.

16. Trace the argument that Henry makes. State the central ideas in this argument, and provide textual evidence to support your assertions.

Paraphrasing the main points or events.	
Interpreting the text.	
Evidence-based response provided.	
Explanatory response provided.	

Write your constructed-response in the box below.

17. Evaluate the argument that Henry makes. Is it effective? Why? Provide textual evidence to support your claims.

Evidence-based response provided.	
Explanatory response provided.	

Write your constructed-response in the box below.

18. What structures does Henry use in order to organize his arguments and ideas? Provide textual evidence to support your analysis of the speech's structure.

Evidence-based response provided.	
Explanatory response provided.	

Write your constructed-response in the box below.

Directions: Read the text. Then answer questions 19-27.

The Secret Garden
by Frances Hodgson Burnett

Chapter I—There Is No One Left

When Mary Lennox was sent to Misselthwaite Manor to live with her uncle everybody said she was the most disagreeable-looking child ever seen. It was true, too. She had a little thin face and a little thin body, thin light hair and a sour expression. Her hair was yellow, and her face was yellow because she had been born in India and had always been ill in one way or another. Her father had held a position under the English Government and had always been busy and ill himself, and her mother had been a great beauty who cared only to go to parties and amuse herself with gay people. She had not wanted a little girl at all, and when Mary was born she handed her over to the care of an Ayah, who was made to understand that if she wished to please the Mem Sahib she must keep the child out of sight as much as possible. So when she was a sickly, fretful, ugly little baby she was kept out of the way, and when she became a sickly, fretful, toddling thing she was kept out of the way also. She never remembered seeing familiarly anything but the dark faces of her Ayah and the other native servants, and as they always obeyed her and gave her her own way in everything, because the Mem Sahib would be angry if she was disturbed by her crying, by the time she was six years old she was as tyrannical and selfish a little pig as ever lived. The young English governess who came to teach her to read and write disliked her so much that she gave up her place in three months, and when other governesses came to try to fill it they always went away in a shorter time than the first one. So if Mary had not chosen to really want to know how to read books she would never have learned her letters at all.

One frightfully hot morning, when she was about nine years old, she awakened feeling very cross, and she became crosser still when she saw that the servant who stood by her bedside was not her Ayah.

"Why did you come?" she said to the strange woman. "I will not let you stay. Send my Ayah to me."

The woman looked frightened, but she only stammered that the Ayah could not come and when Mary threw herself into a passion and beat and kicked her, she looked only more frightened and repeated that it was not possible for the Ayah to come to Missie Sahib.

There was something mysterious in the air that morning. Nothing was done in its regular order and several of the native servants seemed missing, while those whom Mary saw slunk or hurried about with ashy and scared faces. But no one would tell her anything and her Ayah did not come. She was actually left alone as the morning went on, and at last she wandered out into the garden and began to play by herself under a tree near the veranda. She pretended that she was making a flower-bed, and she stuck big scarlet hibiscus blossoms into little heaps of earth, all the time growing more and more angry and muttering to herself the things she would say and the names she would call Saidie when she returned.

"Pig! Pig! Daughter of Pigs!" she said, because to call a native a pig is the worst insult of all.

She was grinding her teeth and saying this over and over again when she heard her mother come out on the veranda with some one. She was with a fair young man and they stood talking together in low strange voices. Mary knew the fair young man who looked like a boy. She had heard that he was a very young officer who had just come from England. The child stared at him, but she stared most at her mother. She always did this when she had a chance to see her, because the Mem Sahib–Mary used to call her that oftener than anything else–was such a tall, slim, pretty person and wore such lovely clothes. Her hair was like curly silk and she had a delicate little nose which seemed to be disdaining things, and she had large laughing eyes. All her clothes were thin and floating, and Mary said they were "full of lace." They looked fuller of lace than ever this morning, but her eyes were not laughing at all. They were large and scared and lifted imploringly to the fair boy officer's face.

"Is it so very bad? Oh, is it?" Mary heard her say.

"Awfully," the young man answered in a trembling voice. "Awfully, Mrs. Lennox. You ought to have gone to the hills two weeks ago."

The Mem Sahib wrung her hands.

"Oh, I know I ought!" she cried. "I only stayed to go to that silly dinner party. What a fool I was!"

At that very moment such a loud sound of wailing broke out from the servants' quarters that she clutched the young man's arm, and Mary stood shivering from head to foot. The wailing grew wilder and wilder. "What is it? What is it?" Mrs. Lennox gasped.

"Some one has died," answered the boy officer. "You did not say it had broken out among your servants."

"I did not know!" the Mem Sahib cried. "Come with me! Come with me!" and she turned and ran into the house.

After that, appalling things happened, and the mysteriousness of the morning was explained to Mary. The cholera had broken out in its most fatal form and people were dying like flies. The Ayah had been taken ill in the night, and it was because she had just died that the servants had wailed in the huts. Before the next day three other servants were dead and others had run away in terror. There was panic on every side, and dying people in all the bungalows.

During the confusion and bewilderment of the second day Mary hid herself in the nursery and was forgotten by everyone. Nobody thought of her, nobody wanted her, and strange things happened of which she knew nothing. Mary alternately cried and slept through the hours. She only knew that people were ill and that she heard mysterious and frightening sounds. Once she crept into the dining-room and found it empty, though a partly finished meal was on the table and chairs and plates looked as if they had been hastily pushed back when the diners rose suddenly for some reason. The child ate some fruit and biscuits, and being thirsty she drank a glass of wine which stood nearly filled. It was sweet, and she did not know how strong it was. Very soon it made her intensely drowsy, and she went back to her nursery and shut herself in again, frightened by cries she heard in the huts and by the hurrying sound of feet. The wine made her so sleepy that she could scarcely keep her eyes open and she lay down on her bed and knew nothing more for a long time.

Many things happened during the hours in which she slept so heavily, but she was not disturbed by the wails and the sound of things being carried in and out of the bungalow.

When she awakened she lay and stared at the wall. The house was perfectly still. She had never known it to be so silent before. She heard neither voices nor footsteps, and wondered if everybody had got well of the cholera and all the trouble was over. She wondered also who would take care of her now her Ayah was dead. There would be a new Ayah, and perhaps she would know some new stories. Mary had been rather tired of the old ones. She did not cry because her nurse had died. She was not an affectionate child and had never cared much for any one. The noise and hurrying about and wailing over the cholera had frightened her, and she had been angry because no one seemed to remember that she was alive. Everyone was too panic-stricken to think of a little girl no one was fond of. When people had the cholera it seemed that they remembered nothing but themselves. But if everyone had got well again, surely some one would remember and come to look for her.

But no one came, and as she lay waiting the house seemed to grow more and more silent. She heard something rustling on the matting and when she looked down she saw a little snake gliding along and watching her with eyes like jewels. She was not frightened, because he was a harmless little thing who would not hurt her and he seemed in a hurry to get out of the room. He slipped under the door as she watched him.

"How queer and quiet it is," she said. "It sounds as if there were no one in the bungalow but me and the snake."

Almost the next minute she heard footsteps in the compound, and then on the veranda. They were men's footsteps, and the men entered the bungalow and talked in low voices. No one went to meet or speak to them and they seemed to open doors and look into rooms. "What desolation!" she heard one voice say. "That pretty, pretty woman! I suppose the child, too. I heard there was a child, though no one ever saw her."

Mary was standing in the middle of the nursery when they opened the door a few minutes later. She looked like an ugly, cross little thing and was frowning because she was beginning to be hungry and feel disgracefully neglected. The first man who came in was a large officer she had once seen talking to her father. He looked tired and troubled, but when he saw her he was so startled that he almost jumped back.

"Barney!" he cried out. "There is a child here! A child alone! In a place like this! Mercy on us, who is she!"

"I am Mary Lennox," the little girl said, drawing herself up stiffly. She thought the man was very rude to call her father's bungalow "A place like this!" "I fell asleep when everyone had the cholera and I have only just wakened up. Why does nobody come?"

"It is the child no one ever saw!" exclaimed the man, turning to his companions. "She has actually been forgotten!"

"Why was I forgotten?" Mary said, stamping her foot. "Why does nobody come?"

The young man whose name was Barney looked at her very sadly. Mary even thought she saw him wink his eyes as if to wink tears away.

"Poor little kid!" he said. "There is nobody left to come."

It was in that strange and sudden way that Mary found out that she had neither father nor mother left; that they had died and been carried away in the night, and that the few native servants who had not died also had left the house as quickly as they could get out of it, none of them even remembering that there was a Missie Sahib. That was why the place was so quiet. It was true that there was no one in the bungalow but herself and the little rustling snake.

19. What does the characterization of Mary Lennox in the first paragraph accomplish? What part of the plot structure is developed from this characterization? Select **two** responses that **best** apply.

☐ A. The characterization of Mary Lennox explains how she was abandoned and how that made her learn how to take care of herself since she was on her own.

☐ B. The characterization of Mary Lennox vividly describes the child and how she became so unpleasant.

☐ C. The characterization of Mary Lennox shows how she was taken care of by the Ayah and how that shaped her into a tolerant child.

☐ D. The characterization of Mary Lennox illustrates how importantly children in this era were treated.

☐ E. The characterization builds the exposition.

☐ F. The characterization builds the denouement.

☐ G. The characterization builds the climax.

20. Using the context of the entire first paragraph, how would you define the word "tyrannical" as it is used in the text?

    O A.   The word tyrannical means "controlling."

    O B.   The word tyrannical means "cruel."

    O C.   The word tyrannical means "unjust."

    O D.   The word tyrannical means "angry."

21. Look at the following sentence:

The woman looked frightened, but she only stammered that the Ayah could not come and when Mary threw herself into a passion and beat and kicked her, she looked only more frightened and repeated that it was not possible for the Ayah to come to Missie Sahib.

Part A

Highlight **two** of the context clues in the sentence that hint at what "stammered" means.

Part B

What does the word "stammered" most likely mean based on the context clues surrounding the word in the sentence? Select **two** responses that **best** apply.

    ☐ A.   The word stammered means "yelled."

    ☐ B.   The word stammered means "speaking demurely."

    ☐ C.   The word stammered means "stuttered."

    ☐ D.   The word stammered means "cried out."

    ☐ E.   The word stammered means "halted speech."

    ☐ F.   The word stammered means "spluttered."

22. Read the following sentence from the passage.

There was something mysterious in the air that morning.

Identify the correct literary element used to advance the story forward. Select **one** response that applies.

- ○ A. The literary element used is an allusion.
- ○ B. The literary element used is foreshadowing.
- ○ C. The literary element used is imagery.
- ○ D. The literary element used is conflict.

23. Read the following description of Mem Sahib-Mary.

Her hair was like curly silk and she had a delicate little nose which seemed to be disdaining things, and she had large laughing eyes.

How does the author use this to develop the story?

- ○ A. The author creates a light mood to offer a break from the negative tone of the narrative.
- ○ B. The author accentuates Mem Sahib-Mary's appearance to demonstrate her fair beauty.
- ○ C. The author contrasts the characterization of Mary Lennox with Mem Sahib-Mary to develop the narrative.
- ○ D. The author builds the central conflict by illustrating the beauty of Mem Sahib-Mary.

24. Look at the following excerpt.

Nobody thought of her, nobody wanted her, and strange things happened of which she knew nothing. Mary alternately cried and slept through the hours. She only knew that people were ill and that she heard mysterious and frightening sounds.

What does it tell the reader about the central conflict? Cite textual evidence that supports your claims.

Paraphrasing the main points or events.	
Interpreting the text.	
Evidence-based response provided.	
Explanatory response provided.	

Write your constructed-response in the box below.

25. Look at the following three sentences.

The house was perfectly still. She had never known it to be so silent before. She heard neither voices nor footsteps, and wondered if everybody had got well of the cholera and all the trouble was over.

How does the current setting foreshadow what has happened?

Evidence-based response provided.	
Explanatory response provided.	

Write your constructed-response in the box below.

26. What is the point of view used in this passage? How does this affect the narrative?

Evidence-based response provided.	
Explanatory response provided.	

Write your constructed-response in the box below.

27. What is a possible theme of this passage? Provide textual evidence to support your theme.

Evidence-based response provided.	
Explanatory response provided.	

Write your constructed-response in the box below.

Directions: Read the text. Then answer questions 28-36.

Symbollic Logic
by Lewis Carroll

"INTRODUCTION"

Source: Carroll, L. (1896). *Symbollic Logic*. New York: Macmillan & Co.

INTRODUCTION.

TO LEARNERS.

The Learner, who wishes to try the question fairly, whether this little book does, or does not, supply the materials for a most interesting mental recreation, is earnestly advised to adopt the following Rules:

(1) Begin at the beginning, and do not allow yourself to gratify a mere idle curiosity by dipping into the book, here and there. This would very likely lead to your throwing it aside, with the remark "This is much too hard for me!, and thus losing the chance of adding a very large item to your stock of mental delights. This Rule (of not dipping) is very desirable with other kinds of books—such as novels, for instance, where you may easily spoil much of the enjoyment you would otherwise get from the story, by dipping into it further on, so that what the author meant to be a pleasant surprise comes to you as a matter of course. Some people, I know, make a practice of looking into Vol. III first, just to see how the story ends: and perhaps it is as well just to know that all ends happily—that the much-persecuted lovers do marry after all, that he is proved to be quite innocent of the murder, that the wicked cousin is completely foiled in his plot and gets the punishment he deserves, and that the rich uncle in India (Qu. Why in India? Ans. Because, somehow, uncles never can get rich anywhere else) dies at exactly the right moment—before taking the trouble to read Vol. I.

This, I say, is just permissible with a novel, where Vol. III has a meaning, even for those who have not read the earlier part of the story; but, with a scientific book, it is sheer insanity: you will find the latter part hopelessly unintelligible, if you read it before reaching it in regular course.

(2) Don't begin any fresh Chapter, or Section, until you are certain that you thoroughly understand the whole book up to that point, and that you have worked, correctly, most if not all of the examples which have been set. So long as you are conscious that all the land you have passed through is absolutely conquered, and that you are leaving no unsolved difficulties behind you, which will be sure to turn up again later on, your triumphal progress will be easy and delightful. Otherwise, you will find your state of puzzlement get worse and worse as you proceed, till you give up the whole thing in utter disgust.

(3) When you come to any passage you don't understand, read it again: if you still don't understand it, read it again: if you fail, even after three readings, very likely your brain is getting a little tired. In that case, put the book away, and take to other occupations, and next day, when you come to it fresh, you will very likely find that it is quite easy.

(4) If possible, find some genial friend, who will read the book along with you, and will talk over the difficulties with you. Talking is a wonderful smoother-over of difficulties. When I come upon anything—in Logic or in any other hard subject—that entirely puzzles me, I find it a capital plan to talk it over, aloud, even when I am all alone. One can explain things so clearly to one's self! And then, you know, one is so patient with one's self: one never gets irritated at one's own stupidity!

If, dear Reader, you will faithfully observe these Rules, and so give my little book a really fair trial, I promise you, most confidently, that you will find Symbollic Logic to be one of the most, if not the most, fascinating of mental recreations! In this First Part, I have carefully avoided all difficulties which seemed to me to be beyond the grasp of an intelligent child of (say) twelve or fourteen years of age. I have myself taught most of its contents, viva voce, to many children, and have found them take a real intelligent interest in the subject. For those, who succeed in mastering Part I, and who begin, like Oliver, "asking for more," I hope to provide, in Part II, some tolerably hard nuts to crack—nuts that will require all the nutcrackers they happen to possess!

Mental recreation is a thing that we all of us need for our mental health; and you may get much healthy enjoyment, no doubt, from Games, such as Back-gammon, Chess, and the new Game "Halma." But, after all, when you have made yourself a first-rate player at any one of these Games, you have nothing real to show for it, as a result! You enjoyed the Game, and the victory, no doubt, at the time: but you have no result that you can treasure up and get real good out of. And, all the while, you have been leaving unexplored a perfect mine of wealth. Once master the machinery of Symbollic Logic, and you have a mental occupation always at hand, of absorbing interest, and one that will be of real use to you in any subject you may take up. It will give you clearness of thought—the ability to see your way through a puzzle—the habit of arranging your ideas in an orderly and get-at-able form—and, more valuable than all, the power to detect fallacies, and to tear to pieces the flimsy illogical arguments, which you will so continually encounter in books, in newspapers, in speeches, and even in sermons, and which so easily delude those who have never taken the trouble to master this fascinating Art. Try it. That is all I ask of you!

L. C.

29, BEDFORD STREET, STRAND.

February 21, 1896.

28. Symbolic logic is a different way of reading. Which of the following responses **best** describes Carroll's perspective on the subject? Select **three** responses that apply.

☐ A. In the introductory paragraph, Carroll refers to symbolic logic as "a most interesting mental recreation."

☐ B. Carroll describes symbolic logic as a way "to see how the story ends."

☐ C. Carroll encourages the reader to work hard in understanding symbolic logic.

☐ D. Carroll mentions how symbolic logic is not for everyone.

☐ E. Carroll emphasizes that there are challenges in this type of reading.

☐ F. Carroll cautions the reader of the importance to quicken the reading pace.

☐ G. Carroll notices how natural symbolic logic reading is.

29. How does Carroll organize the structure of the main part of the Introduction? Select **three** responses that apply.

- ☐ A. Carroll uses numerals to organize the ideas for avoiding confusion from reading symbolic logic.
- ☐ B. Carroll uses numerals to organize specific reading strategies that may be used to read symbolic logic.
- ☐ C. Carroll breaks up the Introduction into paragraphs to explain how symbolic logic can offer "mental delights."
- ☐ D. Carroll uses paragraphing to set off important details in his text to explain how to understand symbolic logic.
- ☐ E. Carroll uses argumentation to prove his point.
- ☐ F. Carroll offers suggestions in reading symbolic logic.
- ☐ G. Carroll provides an anecdote to emphasize his point.

30. What is the central idea in the first suggestion that Carroll offers? Select **two** responses that **best** apply.

- ☐ A. Carroll explains how reading the story at the end may work for regular reading, but it will not work for symbolic logic.
- ☐ B. Carroll describes how different symbolic logic is from the normal way of reading a fictional narrative.
- ☐ C. Carroll urges the reader to start at the beginning and avoid looking ahead to the end or to any other parts of the story due to the nature of symbolic logic.
- ☐ D. Carroll cautions the reader about losing the chance to read symbolic logic if the rules are not followed.
- ☐ E. Carroll chastises some ineffective readers.
- ☐ F. Carroll suggests skipping symbolic logic if the reader is not patient.

31. Look at the following excerpt from the passage.

So long as you are conscious that all the land you have passed through is absolutely conquered….

What does Carroll mean by the figurative language about the land? Select **two** responses that **best** apply.

☐ A. Carroll is comparing the second reading strategy to a conquered land where the reader understands the message of the story.

☐ B. Carroll is comparing this reading strategy to a land where there is a vast amount of information to be gained.

☐ C. Carroll is comparing the second reading strategy to a land of confusion.

☐ D. Carroll is comparing this reading strategy to a land that is waiting to be conquered.

☐ E. Carroll is using the idea of a conquered land to symbolize mastery.

☐ F. Carroll is stating that there is a whole frontier ahead for the reader of symbolic logic.

32. What is the central idea of the third strategy? Select **all** that apply.

☐ A. The central idea is that readers must reread the story whenever there is an obstacle in understanding the story.

☐ B. The central idea is that brains get tired and need to rest in order to read symbolic logic effectively.

☐ C. The central idea is that a mind must be fresh and alert in order to reread and to understand troubling parts of the story.

☐ D. The central idea is to reread any parts of the story that are hard to understand.

☐ E. The central idea is to persevere and continue reading on.

☐ F. The central idea is to move at a swift pace when tired.

33. What are some of the main arguments that Carroll makes for the enjoyment of symbolic logic reading? Select **three** responses that **best** apply.

☐ A. Carroll argues that it is an enjoyable type of reading.

☐ B. Carroll argues that even children can enjoy this type of writing and that this reading can challenge the mind and bring clarity of thought.

☐ C. Carroll argues that this type of reading can help children do better in academics if they learn how to do this type of reading.

☐ D. Carroll argues that this is an art that should not go unnoticed by potential readers.

☐ E. Carroll argues that this kind of reading is not for everyone.

☐ F. Carroll argues that symbolic logic is a challenging pastime.

☐ G. Carroll argues that this is a leisurely activity.

34. What is the central idea of this entire passage? Include textual evidence to support your claims.

Paraphrasing the main points or events.	
Interpreting the text.	
Evidence-based response provided.	
Explanatory response provided.	

Write your constructed-response in the box below.

35. Write a five-sentence objective summary that describes the key points in this passage.

Evidence-based response provided.	
Explanatory response provided.	

Write your constructed-response in the box below.

36. What is Carroll's purpose for writing this Introduction? Include textual evidence to support your assertions.

Evidence-based response provided.	
Explanatory response provided.	

Write your constructed-response in the box below.

(Answers are on pages 156–161.)

Performance Task—Part One

Directions: After reviewing the following three sources, you will answer questions and write a narrative essay. Briefly scan the sources and questions that follow before beginning your close read of the three sources.

Source #1

"The Poetic Principle"
by Edgar Allan Poe

Source: Poe, E. A. (1903). *The Works of Edgar Allan Poe, The Raven Edition, Volume 5.* New York: P. F. Collier and Son.

In speaking of the Poetic Principle, I have no design to be either thorough or profound. While discussing, very much at random, the essentiality of what we call Poetry, my principal purpose will be to cite for consideration, some few of those minor English or American poems which best suit my own taste, or which, upon my own fancy, have left the most definite impression. By "minor poems" I mean, of course, poems of little length. And here, in the beginning, permit me to say a few words in regard to a somewhat peculiar principle, which, whether rightfully or wrongfully, has always had its influence in my own critical estimate of the poem. I hold that a long poem does not exist. I maintain that the phrase, "a long poem," is simply a flat contradiction in terms.

I need scarcely observe that a poem deserves its title only inasmuch as it excites, by elevating the soul. The value of the poem is in the ratio of this elevating excitement. But all excitements are, through a psychal necessity, transient. That degree of excitement which would entitle a poem to be so called at all, cannot be sustained throughout a composition of any great length. After the lapse of half an hour, at the very utmost, it flags—fails—a revulsion ensues—and then the poem is, in effect, and in fact, no longer such.

There are, no doubt, many who have found difficulty in reconciling the critical dictum that the "Paradise Lost" is to be devoutly admired throughout, with the absolute impossibility of maintaining for it, during perusal, the amount of enthusiasm which that critical dictum would demand. This great work, in fact, is to be regarded as poetical, only when, losing sight of that vital requisite in all works of Art, Unity, we view it merely as a series of minor poems. If, to preserve its Unity—its totality of effect or impression—we read it (as would be necessary) at a single sitting, the result is but a constant alternation of excitement and depression. After a passage of what we feel to be true poetry, there follows, inevitably, a passage of platitude which no critical prejudgment can force us to admire; but if, upon completing the work, we read it again, omitting the first book—that is to say, commencing with the second—we shall be surprised at now finding that admirable which we before condemned—that damnable which we had previously so much admired. It follows from all this that the ultimate, aggregate, or absolute effect of even the best epic under the sun, is a nullity:—and this is precisely the fact.

In regard to the Iliad, we have, if not positive proof, at least very good reason for believing it intended as a series of lyrics; but, granting the epic intention, I can say only that the work is based in an imperfect sense of art. The modern epic is, of the supposititious ancient model, but an inconsiderate and blindfold imitation. But the day of these artistic anomalies is over. If, at any time, any very long poem were popular in reality, which I doubt, it is at least clear that no very long poem will ever be popular again.

That the extent of a poetical work is, ceteris paribus, the measure of its merit, seems undoubtedly, when we thus state it, a proposition sufficiently absurd—yet we are indebted for it to the Quarterly Reviews. Surely there can be nothing in mere size, abstractly considered—there can be nothing in mere bulk, so far as a volume is concerned, which has so continuously elicited admiration from these saturnine pamphlets! A mountain, to be sure, by the mere sentiment of physical magnitude which it conveys, does impress us with a sense of the sublime—but no man is impressed after this fashion by the material grandeur of even "The Columbiad." Even the Quarterlies have not instructed us to be so impressed by it. As yet, they have not insisted on our estimating "Lamar" tine by the cubic foot, or Pollock by the pound— but what else are we to infer from their continual plating about "sustained effort"? If, by "sustained effort," any little gentleman has accomplished an epic, let us frankly commend him for the effort—if this indeed be a thing conk mendable—but let us forbear praising the epic on the effort's account. It is to be hoped that common sense, in the time to come, will prefer deciding upon a work of Art rather by the impression it makes—by the effect it produces— than by the time it took to impress the effect, or by the amount of "sustained effort" which had been found necessary in effecting the impression. The fact is, that perseverance is one thing and genius quite another—nor can all the Quarterlies in Christendom confound them. By and by, this proposition, with many which I have been just urging, will be received as self-evident. In the meantime, by being generally condemned as falsities, they will not be essentially damaged as truths.

On the other hand, it is clear that a poem may be improperly brief. Undue brevity degenerates into mere epigrammatism. A very short poem, while now and then producing a brilliant or vivid, never produces a profound or enduring effect. There must be the steady pressing down of the stamp upon the wax. De Beranger has wrought innumerable things, pungent and spirit-stirring, but in general they have been too imponderous to stamp themselves deeply into the public attention, and thus, as so many feathers of fancy, have been blown aloft only to be whistled down the wind.

Source #2

Preface to *A Study of Poetry*
by Bliss Perry

The method of studying poetry which I have followed in this book was sketched some years ago in my chapter on "Poetry" in *Counsel Upon the Reading of Books*. My confidence that the genetic method is the natural way of approaching the subject has been shared by many lovers of poetry. I hope, however, that I have not allowed my insistence upon the threefold process of "impression, transforming imagination, and expression" to harden into a set formula. Formulas have a certain dangerous usefulness for critics and teachers, but they are a very small part of one's training in the appreciation of poetry.

I have allotted little or no space to the specific discussion of epic and drama, as these types are adequately treated in many books. Our own generation is peculiarly attracted by various forms of the lyric, and in Part Two I have devoted especial attention to that field.

While I hope that the book may attract the traditional "general reader," I have also tried to arrange it in such a fashion that it may be utilized in the classroom. I have therefore ventured, in the Notes and Illustrations and Appendix, to suggest some methods and material for the use of students.

I wish to express my obligations to Professor R. M. Alden, whose *Introduction to Poetry* and *English Verse* I have used in my own Harvard courses in poetry. His views of metre have probably influenced mine even more than

I am aware. The last decade, which has witnessed such an extraordinary revival of interest in poetry, has produced many valuable contributions to poetic theory. I have found Professor Fairchild's *Making of Poetry* particularly suggestive. Attention is called, in the Notes and Bibliography, to many other recent books on the subject.

Professors A. S. Cook of Yale and F. B. Snyder of Northwestern University have been kind enough to read in manuscript certain chapters of this book, and Dr. P. F. Baum of Harvard has assisted me most courteously. I am indebted to several fellow-writers for their consent to the use of extracts from their books, particularly to Brander Matthews for a passage from *These Many Years* and to Henry Osborn Taylor for a passage from his *Classical Heritage of the Middle Ages*.

I wish also to thank the publishers who have generously allowed me to use brief quotations from copyrighted books, especially Henry Holt & Co. for permission to use a quotation and drawing from William James's *Psychology*, and The Macmillan Company for permission to borrow from John La Farge's delightful *Considerations on Painting*.

B. P.

Source #3

A Study of Poetry
by Bliss Perry

Part I: Poetry in General

Chapter I

A GLANCE AT THE BACKGROUND

It is a gray day in autumn. I am sitting at my desk, wondering how to begin the first chapter of this book about poetry. Outside the window a woman is contentedly kneeling on the upturned brown earth of her tulip-bed, patting lovingly with her trowel as she covers the bulbs for next spring's blossoming. Does she know Katharine Tynan's verses about "Planting Bulbs"? Probably not. But I find myself dropping the procrastinating pen, and murmuring some of the lines:

"Setting my bulbs a-row
  In cold earth under the grasses,
Till the frost and the snow
  Are gone and the Winter passes—
"Turning the sods and the clay
  I think on the poor sad people
Hiding their dead away
  In the churchyard, under the steeple.
"All poor women and men,
  Broken-hearted and weeping,
Their dead they call on in vain,
  Quietly smiling and sleeping.
"Friends, now listen and hear,
  Give over crying and grieving,
There shall come a day and a year
  When the dead shall be as the living.
"There shall come a call, a foot-fall,
  And the golden trumpeters blowing
Shall stir the dead with their call,
  Bid them be rising and going.
"Then in the daffodil weather,
  Lover shall run to lover;
Friends all trooping together;
  Death and Winter be over.
"Laying my bulbs in the dark,
  Visions have I of hereafter.
Lip to lip, breast to breast, hark!
  No more weeping, but laughter!"

Yet this is no way to start your chapter, suggests Conscience. Why do you not write an opening paragraph, for better for worse, instead of looking out of the window and quoting Katharine Tynan? And then it flashes over me, in lieu of answer, that I have just discovered one way of beginning the chapter, after all! For what I should like to do in this book is to set forth in decent prose some of the strange potencies of verse: its power, for instance, to seize upon a physical image like that of a woman planting bulbs, and transmute it into a symbol of the resurrection of the dead; its capacity for turning fact into truth and brown earth into beauty; for remoulding the broken syllables of human speech into sheer music; for lifting the mind, bowed down by wearying thought and haunting fear, into a brooding ecstasy wherein weeping is changed into laughter and autumnal premonitions of death into assurance of life, and the narrow paths of individual experience are widened into those illimitable spaces where the imagination rules. Poetry does all this, assuredly. But how? And why? That is our problem.

"The future of poetry is immense," declared Matthew Arnold, and there are few lovers of literature who doubt his triumphant assertion. But the past of poetry is immense also: impressive in its sheer bulk and in its immemorial duration. At a period earlier than any recorded history, poetry seems to have occupied the attention of men, and some of the finest spirits in every race that has attained to civilization have devoted themselves to its production, or at least given themselves freely to the enjoyment of reciting and reading verse, and of meditating upon its significance. A consciousness of this rich human background should accompany each new endeavor to examine the facts about poetry and to determine its essential nature. The facts are indeed somewhat complicated, and the nature of poetry, in certain aspects of it, at least, will remain as always a mystery. Yet in that very complication and touch of mystery there is a fascination which has laid its spell upon countless generations of men, and which has been deepened rather than destroyed by the advance of science and the results of scholarship. The study of folklore and comparative literature has helped to explain some of the secrets of poetry; the psychological laboratory, the history of criticism, the investigation of linguistics, the modern developments in music and the other arts, have all contributed something to our intelligent enjoyment of the art of poetry and to our sense of its importance in the life of humanity. There is no field of inquiry where the interrelations of knowledge are more acutely to be perceived. The beginner in the study of poetry may at once comfort himself and increase his zest by remembering that any real training which he has already had in scientific observation, in the habit of analysis, in the study of races and historic periods, in the use of languages, in the practice or interpretation of any of the fine arts, or even in any bodily exercise that has developed his sense of rhythm, will be of ascertainable value to him in this new study.

But before attempting to apply his specific knowledge or aptitude to the new field for investigation, he should be made aware of some of the wider questions which the study of poetry involves. The first of these questions has to do with the relations of the study of poetry to the general field of Aesthetics.

Directions: Answer the following questions based on the **three** sources you just read and prepare to take the second part of this performance task. Your responses will be scored.

1. Write a summary of source #1. Include textual evidence to support your central ideas and details. Try to encapsulate the ideas of Poe on the subject of poetry.

   Write your response here in the box below.

2. What are the key impressions of Poe and Perry on the effects of poetry? Use textual evidence from at least **two** sources that support your assertions.

Write your constructed-response here in the box below.

3. Compare and contrast the perspectives of Poe and Perry. Use textual evidence from **two or more** sources that support the similarities and differences.

Write your constructed-response here in the box below.

(Answers are on page 162.)

Performance Task—Part Two: Poetry Narrative

Task: A poetry contest was held at your school district, and now there is going to be a writing reception ceremony where the winners are going to read their poetry and receive their awards. In the program for this event, your school is adding the reading of a fictional narrative that will express the power of poetry. You are charged with the challenge to write this fictional narrative based on three sources that you have gathered during your research process.

Your Assignment: You will now plan, draft, revise, and edit a multi-paragraph fictional narrative that expresses the power of poetry. Be sure to include the setting, character development, plot, dialogue, and descriptive language in your story.

Poetry Narrative Scoring

1. **Organization/Purpose**—Is there an effective plot that creates unity throughout the story? Is there an established setting, characters, and point of view? Are there effective uses of transitions? Is the organization of the story logical? Is it appropriate for the audience? Is there a purpose?

2. **Development/Elaboration**—Is there effective elaboration with details, dialogue, and description? Are characters, setting, and events clearly developed? Are there connections to the source materials? Are there sensory details, figurative language, and narrative techniques employed in the story? Is the style effective?

3. **Conventions**—Is there effective use of correct sentence structure, punctuation, capitalization, grammar, and spelling throughout the narrative?

Directions: Plan, draft, revise, and edit a multi-paragraph fictional narrative that uses the sources from Part 1 and that addresses all parts of the writing task. Write your paragraph in the box below.

(Answers are on pages 163–164.)

Answers Explained

In this chapter, you will find sample answers to the On Your Own practice questions and the practice test from Chapter 6. For the English Language Arts Practice Test, there are answers to the selected-response tasks or questions. There are full samples for 2, 1, or 0 point constructed-response items. Finally, there are performance task responses to both parts. Part 2 also includes a 4, 3, 2, or 1 sample response. Compare your answers and see how you did.

Chapter 2: Selected-Response Tasks (Multiple-Choice)

Selected-Response Items, Passage 1—Narrative, pages 14–16

1. **Correct Answers: (A)** The setting introduces the main characters and describes the personalities of the characters. **(G)** The setting advances the plot with a conflict in the "Law of the Jungle."

   Rationale: These responses describe how the setting shapes both the characters and the plot. It explains what the setting specifically does in order to develop characterization and plot in the story.

2. **Correct Answers: (C)** The author describes Tabaqui, the jackal, with details that tell the reader what he is likely to think as he is characterized as unpredictable. **(E)** Father Wolf has an opposing point of view to Tabaqui, and the author contrasts these points of view.

   Rationale: These responses show how Tabaqui and Father Wolf are characterized and how that affects their points of view. It then states how these opposing views are contrasted with one another in order to develop the plot of the narrative.

3. **Correct Answer: (B)** The author has developed this character throughout the passage, and he portrays this character with consistency as Tabaqui makes the comment about Shere Khan to upset Father Wolf, which sets up the theme.

Rationale: This response reiterates the importance of Tabaqui as a character that affects the plot of the story, that adds conflict to the story, and that contributes to the theme of the narrative. This makes Tabaqui an important character.

4. **Correct Answers:** Tabaqui runs about making mischief, telling tales, eating rags and pieces of leather from the village rubbish-heaps.

   Rationale: Despise means to dislike, so these are things that Tabaqui does to make the other characters despise him. They serve as context clues to demonstrate negative connotations.

5. **Correct Answers: (A)** run **(D)** scurry

   Rationale: Scuttle means to run quickly, so run or scurry are synonyms, or words that have similar meanings.

6. **Correct Answers:** Tabaqui knew as well as anyone else that there is nothing so unlucky as to compliment children to their faces. It pleased him to see Mother and Father Wolf look uncomfortable.

   Rationale: These two sentences demonstrate the joy that Tabaqui gets from causing mischief. They support this assertion about Tabaqui's character.

7. **Correct Answer: (B)** search fervently

   Rationale: Scouring the jungle means that they were searching very fervently for this character.

Selected-Response Items, Passage 2—Nonfiction, pages 18–20

8. **Correct Answers: (B)** Developing as a student into a man is a complex process that requires thought and hard work. **(E)** Reflection is a part of this process as the author contemplates how his younger years shaped his life. **(F)** It is the obstacles that make people who they are.

   Rationale: These are the best responses because they most completely encapsulate the central ideas of the passage. The author is very contemplative and reflective about his life. This is the "take away" of the passage.

9. **Correct Answers: (A)** The author provides details about his class rivals to illustrate how school from his younger days taught him how to endure. **(B)** Military school provided structure and discipline to the author. **(C)** His idea of somnambulism, or sleepwalking, adds charm to the author's account of his

reflective and contemplative nature as a young man. **(D)** He reminisces about the knot-hole to show how school was very challenging.

Rationale: These details describe the author's experiences that best support the central ideas in the passage. Class rivalry and somnambulism add details to the events in the author's life that are most important and central to his formative years.

10. **Correct Answer: (C)** The author uses similes to characterize his early school rival in a way that adds interest and a colorful description that would otherwise be less effective.

Rationale: This response identifies specific uses of figurative language and explains how this particular language enhances the meaning of the text and the central ideas that go with it.

11. **Correct Answers: (A)** figurative language, **(B)** hyperbole, and **(C)** imagery

Rationale: To "soak my system" is an example of figurative language, specifically imagery, that exaggerates the inundation of "hard words and information."

12. **Correct Answer: (C)** feel uncertain

Rationale: The author claims that he felt uncertain without his safe knot-hole.

13. **Correct Answers:** feet like a summer squash and eyes like those of a dead codfish

Rationale: Similes are comparisons between two unlike things using *like* or *as*.

14. **Correct Answers: (E)** I was never so ashamed in my life. **(F)** Mine is but the history of one who struggled on year after year, trying to do better, but most always failing to connect.

Rationale: The author was ashamed of his somnambulism, which shows challenge as well as struggling each year, but failing.

On Your Own, Selected-Response Items, Passage 3—Nonfiction, pages 22–25

15. **Correct Answer: (B)** The author expresses how women are a valid group in the country that has not been permitted to exercise a right that is supported by the U.S. Constitution—voting.

Rationale: The author definitely reiterates injustice and focuses on equality for all of humanity.

16. **Correct Answers: (C)** The author is using comparative language to enhance an effect of strong persuasion from exaggeration. **(E)** The author is using repetition to communicate a point that supports the central idea of her speech.

    Rationale: The comparative language, exaggeration, and repetition help structure an effective argument to enhance the amount of persuasion.

17. **Correct Answers: (B)** The author uses this language to communicate how only a bold and daring human would disagree that women are persons. **(C)** The author embeds this word within the argument that women are persons, which makes the opponents seem unreasonable.

    Rationale: The author uses the word "hardihood" to illustrate how opponents are unfairly bold about not permitting women to vote.

18. **Correct Answer for Part A: (A)** In her speech, Susan B. Anthony expresses the need for justice and equality for all of humanity.

    Rationale: This thesis makes an effective assertion about the underlying meaning of the speech.

    Correct Answers for Part B: (A) The preamble of the Federal Constitution says: "We, the people of the United States, in order to form a more perfect union, establish justice...." **(B)** And we formed it, not to give the blessings of liberty, but to secure them; not to the half of ourselves and the half of our posterity, but to the whole people—women as well as men. **(C)** It was we, the people; not we, the white male citizens; nor yet we, the male citizens; but we, the whole people, who formed the Union. **(D)** And it is a downright mockery to talk to women of their enjoyment of the blessings of liberty while they are denied the use of the only means of securing them provided by this democratic-republican government—the ballot.

    Rationale: These sentences support that justice and equality are the central ideas and most important details in the entire speech.

19. **Correct Answers: (C)** future generations of people **(F)** future women

    Rationale: The word "posterity" means that future women and future generations of people will be burdened with a lack of voting rights.

Chapter 3: Constructed-Response Tasks

On Your Own, Passage 5—Nonfiction, pages 67–68

1. **Answers will vary.** Below is a sample with a 2, 1, or 0 constructed-response with rationale.

   2—The statement by Dryden means that the observation of the beauty seen in the lands becomes a part of the human experience of being an individual within this beauty. This relates to the central theme because the features such as this "river is not laid down on any map which" the author has seen demonstrates how vast and beautiful this land in California really is in its majestic nature.

   Rationale: This response addresses all of the parts of the question and includes textual evidence to support the writer's assertions.

   1—This statement means that the land of California is beautiful, which relates to the central theme in that humanity can revel in nature's beauty.

   Rationale: This response addresses all of the parts of the question; however, textual evidence is missing.

   0—There is beauty here.

   Rationale: This response touches vaguely on the question with no textual evidence.

2. **Answers will vary.** Below is a sample with a 2, 1, or 0 constructed-response with rationale.

   2—The purpose of including Dr. Marsh's description of California is to offer testimony of how beautiful the land of California is as it has a "noble valley...the great Snowy Mountains...broad and fertile valleys."

   Rationale: This response thoroughly explains the purpose of Dr. Marsh's description and includes textual evidence.

   1—The purpose of including Dr. Marsh's description is to show how beautiful and amazing California is with all of its splendor in the lands.

   Rationale: This response offers purpose with no textual evidence.

   0—The purpose is to show things.

   Rationale: This response does not answer the question and does not include textual evidence.

3. **Answers will vary.** Below is a sample with a 2, 1, or 0 constructed-response with rationale.

2—The underlying meaning of this passage is to embrace the beauty of the California lands and to feel the transcendental quality of nature. Dr. Marsh supports this as he describes "a well-timbered stream" that "flows through a country of great fertility and beauty."

Rationale: This response completely answers the question and provides ample support to add validity to the assertions.

1—The underlying meaning is that there is a "great range of the Snowy Mountains" along with "agricultural resources of California."

Rationale: There is textual evidence for support, but no statement of the underlying meaning.

0—The underlying meaning is central.

Rationale: This response does not include any possible answers to the questions and has no textual evidence.

Chapter 4: Performance Task Items

Performance Task—Part One, pages 79-80

1. **Answers will vary.** Below is a sample with a 2, 1, or 0 possible performance task response.

2—Physical activity is important, and young people should follow physical activity guidelines because it helps in improving "strength and endurance… healthy bones and muscles…helps control weight." Another source recognizes how it "may reduce anxiety and depression and promote positive mental health.

1—Young people should follow the guidelines for physical activity because it "reduces anxiety and stress, increases self-esteem, and may improve blood pressure and cholesterol levels."

0—Physical activity is important for young people because it "helps control weight."

2. **Answers will vary.** Below is a sample with a 2, 1, or 0 possible performance task response.

2—Schools definitely have a role in this issue as they "should ensure that physical education is provided to all students in all grades and is taught by qualified teachers." Furthermore, schools with "physical activity programs benefit communities as well as students and schools."

1—Schools help young people "get physical and mental health benefits" and "benefit communities as well as students."

0—Schools should help young people with physical activity because it helps them.

3. **Answers will vary.** Below is a sample with a 2, 1, or 0 possible performance task response.

2—Although the sources have some conflicting facts such as percentages of students who exercise a certain amount, there are many commonalities as well. At most, "27.1% of high school students surveyed had participated in at least 60 minutes per day...on all 7 days." A different source had it at "17%." Benefits include muscle-strengthening and bone-strengthening. Consequences include obesity and high blood pressure.

1—There is differing factual information from all three sources. Few high school students exercise for at least 60 minutes per day for all seven days. Benefits include higher academic achievement and muscle-strengthening.

0—There are differences in the factual information. There are benefits and consequences in all three of the sources.

Performance Task—Part Two, pages 81–83

Argumentative Writing

Answers will vary. Below are samples with a 4, 3, 2, or 1 rubric response.

Rubric Score 4

Do we need to increase physical activity in young people in this country? Should schools play a role in promoting healthy physical activity? The evidence does suggest that physical activity in young people should increase and that schools have a vital role in encouraging students to get healthier. Among all three sources, it is clear that 29% at most "of high school students had participated in at least 60 minutes per day...on each of the 7 days." (Source #1)

The benefits and consequences are clear, and the role of schools should be a focal point of this issue.

There are many benefits and consequences that go with good or lacking physical activity in young people. Benefits include building and maintaining "healthy bones and muscles," reducing "the risk of developing...chronic diseases," and improving "students' academic performance." (Source #1) Consequences include "obesity...dying prematurely...of heart disease, and...developing diabetes, colon cancer, and high blood pressure." (Source #1)

Some people may say that "77% of children aged 9-13 years reported participaing in free-time physical activity during the previous 7 days"; however, it is clear that "physical activity declines as young people age." (Source #1) According to Source #2, "...the U.S. Department of Health and Human Services, recommend that children and adolescents aged 6-17 years should have 60 minutes...or more of physical activity each day."

Source #3 states that schools "...are an ideal setting for teaching youth how to adopt and maintain a healthy, active lifestyle. Schools can help youth learn how to be physically active for a lifetime." Furthermore, youth "get physical and mental health benefits"; thorough "school-based physical activity programs can help youth meet most of their physical activity needs"; and schools can "benefit communities as well as students." (Source #3)

According to the facts from these sources, it is clear that young people between the ages of 6 and 17 need to increase their physical activity in the United States. The benefits and consequences are clear. Opposing viewpoints about 9- to 13-year-olds getting enough activity do not discount the young people who really need an increase in physical activity. Finally, schools have a significant role in making this happen for youngsters in this nation.

Rubric Score 3

Physical activity in young people is so important. Many "high school students surveyed had [not] participated in at least 60 minutes per day [in] physical activity on all 7 days before the survey." (Source #1) There are many benefits to physical activity in youngsters, and opposing viewpoints may say that it is adequate, but it is not. Also, schools should play a role in increasing physical activity.

Benefits include reducing "the risk of developing obesity, lessening "feelings of depression and anxiety," and improving "academic performance." (Source #1) This proves that there are many bene ts to higher physical activity in young people.

Some opposing viewpoints may include that "77% of children aged 9-13 years reported participating in free-time physical activity during the previous 7 days." (Source #1) However, "only 17% of 9th-12th grade students said they were physically active at least 60 minutes per day." (Source #3)

Schools can do a lot to encourage young people to exercise. They may have "policies that provide time for organized physical activity and free play"; include "information to parents about the benefits of physical activity"; and promote "families and local groups to be involved in school-based physical activities and events." (Source #3)

It is clear how important physical activity is to young people in this nation. There are benefits despite the opposing viewpoints that say physical activity is adequate based on a few facts. Schools should play an important role in encouraging more physical activity in their young people. This is a significant part of a child's young life.

Rubric Score 2

There are many reasons why young peple should exercise. They need to "build and maintain healthy bones and muscles." This is imprtant. Schools should help. They should do things that wil help students exercise more.

When peple work out, they can lessen being obese and avoid diseses like diabetes. They can do beter in school and spend more time being healthy.

Schols should help a lot. They can have classes that make more physical activity in their students. This will help a lot with everything.

Young peple should work out. It helps them a lost. Schols can help by adding classes that make students do active things.

Rubric Score 1

Children should do fisicle activity. They can do better in health. They can have "healthy bones and muscles." They can not be overwait. Schools can help. They can mak it so the students want to play a lot more. it is a good thing fore eveyone.

Chapter 6: Practice Test

Computer-Adaptive Test, pages 97–135

1. **Correct Answers: (A)** Lofty means elevated at a higher level. **(E)** Lofty means of a great height.

2. **Correct Answers: (B)** The author wants to set the tone of the story. **(E)** The stern and sturdy land describes a stern and sturdy tone. **(F)** The words stern and sturdy focus the reader on the strength of the land.

3. **Correct Answers: (C)** The introduction of each character builds reader interest as it talks about the grueling trip. **(E)** The introduction of each character builds reader interest as it describes an unusual situation in how the child is dressed. **(F)** The exposition of the plot structure is introduced. **(G)** The introduction of the characters builds reader interest by including some dialogue.

4. **Correct Answers: Bold sections should be circled for Part A.** She did not look more than five years old, if as much, but what her natural figure was like, it would have been hard to say, for **she had apparently two, if not three dresses, one above the other, and over these a thick red woollen shawl wound round about her**, so that the little body presented a shapeless appearance, as, with its **small feet shod in thick, nailed mountain-shoes**, it slowly and laboriously plodded its way up in the heat.

Correct Answer for Part B: (B) The young girl was dressed heavily, so "laboriously plodded" must mean working hard at walking like dragging her feet with a lot of weight.

5. **Answers will vary.** Below is a sample with a 2, 1, or 0 constructed-response.

2—The exchange of dialogue between Dete and Barbel reveals that there may be a conflict with Alm-Uncle watching the young child as Barbel exclaims that Dete "must be out of your [her] senses." This builds the rising action of the plot structure.

1—Barbel explains how Dete does "know what he is." Alm-Uncle may not be fit to watch the child.

0—The dialogue is interesting about Alm-Uncle.

6. **Answers will vary.** Below is a sample with a 2, 1, or 0 constructed-response.

2—The point of view used in this passage is third person point of view which affects the character development because it allows the reader to see multiple character perspectives.

1—The point of view used is third person point of view because of the pronouns used such as "he" and "she."

0—The point of view tells the reader about the characters.

7. **Answers will vary.** Below is a sample with a 2, 1, or 0 constructed-response.

2—The author contrasts the points of view of Dete and Barbel through dialogue. Dete wants to live a better life which means dropping the child with Alm-Uncle, whereas Barbel thinks Alm-Uncle is unfit to watch the child. This tells the reader that Dete is selfish and that Barbel is concerned. This advances the plot structure in the rising action.

1—Dete is selfish, and Barbel is a gossip, which is shown through the dialogue.

0—Both characters like to talk.

8. **Answers will vary.** Below is a sample with a 2, 1, or 0 constructed-response.

2—The author characterizes Alm-Uncle as a "misanthrope" who "will have nothing to do with anybody" and who "never sets his foot inside a church." Alm-Uncle sounds like a hermit who is not socially acceptable.

1—Alm-Uncle is a strange person who does not like to socialize with other people.

0—He is a weak person.

9. **Answers will vary.** Below is a sample with a 2, 1, or 0 constructed-response.

2—A possible theme is that people must make the best of their situation and develop as humans regardless of life's circumstances.

1—A possible theme is be strong.

0—There is trouble.

10. **Correct Answers: (A)** Henry is ensuring that he does not offend his fellow brethren in the House. **(C)** Henry is setting up his argument by first commending his adversaries to prepare them for his argument.

11. **Correct Answers: (A)** This sentence is a claim, or position, that Henry is stating. **(D)** This is an argument that Henry is setting up for his speech.

12. **Correct Answers: (D)** Henry establishes the need for dialogue in order to find truth. **(E)** Henry states the gravity of the topic. **(G)** Henry appeals to the emotions of his opponents.

13. **Correct Answers: (C)** Henry is stating that it is easy for men to hope for the best, which deludes and does not resolve the problem. **(E)** Henry is emphasizing that hope will not help in this situation. **(F)** Henry cautions his brethren about false hope.

14. **Correct Answer: (B)** Henry uses the image of "chains" to explain how England has imprisoned this country.

15. **Correct Answers: (D)** Henry is using the storm as a symbol of the turmoil and fighting that is imminent. **(F)** Henry is using figurative language to make an effective point.

16. **Answers will vary.** Below is a sample with a 2, 1, or 0 constructed-response.

    2—Henry begins his argument by stating that "different men often see the same subject in different lights." The central ideas in his argument are that man cannot "indulge in the illusions of hope." Instead, he concludes that "we must fight." Inaction will only bring imprisonment.

    1—Henry states that not fighting is "treason towards" the "country." Furthermore, he warns against seeing and hearing not if no war happens.

    0—Henry wants to fight.

17. **Answers will vary.** Below is a sample with a 2, 1, or 0 constructed-response.

    2—Henry's argument is effective because he characterizes the situation with beautiful language such as talking about "illusions of hope." He repeats how they have been insulted, "disregarded," and "spurned." The only option is to "fight."

    1—Henry uses many argumentative strategies to appeal to the emotions of his listeners.

    0—Henry is angry.

18. **Answers will vary.** Below is a sample with a 2, 1, or 0 constructed-response.

    2—The general structure of Henry's speech includes providing a beginning, middle, and end. Furthermore, Henry frames his arguments with relevant questions such as "Are fleets and armies necessary to a work of love and reconciliation?" and "Shall we try argument?"

    1—Henry includes an introduction, a body, and a conclusion in the structure of his speech.

    0—Henry works hard to convince people of things.

19. **Correct Answers: (B)** The characterization of Mary Lennox vividly describes the child and how she became so unpleasant. **(E)** The characterization builds the exposition.

20. **Correct Answer: (A)** The word tyrannical means "controlling."

21. **Correct Answer for Part A in bold: The woman looked frightened**, but she only stammered that the Ayah could not come and when Mary threw herself into a passion and beat and kicked her, **she looked only more frightened and repeated that it was not possible for the Ayah to come to Missie Sahib.**

    Correct Answers for Part B: (E) The word stammered means "halted speech." **(F)** The word stammered means "spluttered."

22. **Correct Answer: (B)** The literary element used is foreshadowing.

23. **Correct Answer: (C)** The author contrasts the characterization of Mary Lennox with Mem Sahib-Mary to develop the narrative.

24. **Answers will vary.** Below is a sample with a 2, 1, or 0 constructed-response.

    2—The excerpt illustrates how the child of Mary Lennox is neglected and not cared for as "nobody wanted her." This hints that the true, central conflict is about the consequences of abandonment as Mary Lennox goes through a journey to become a better person.

    1—The central conflict is the illness that plagues the household as Mary Lennox is forgotten.

    0—There are problems for the child.

25. **Answers will vary.** Below is a sample with a 2, 1, or 0 constructed-response.

    2—The current setting where the child is bathed in silence foreshadows that the child will find out something dark and sad as she moves forward in the story.

    1—The current setting will find the child in the capable hands of someone else who will save her from her problems.

    0—The setting is silent.

26. **Answers will vary.** Below is a sample with a 2, 1, or 0 constructed-response.

    2—The point of view used in this passage is third person point of view, which affects the narrative in that it reveals the thoughts and feelings of all the characters which adds dimension to the story.

1—The passage is in third person point of view, which relates the thoughts of all the characters.

0—The story is about a girl.

27. **Answers will vary.** Below is a sample with a 2, 1, or 0 constructed-response.

2—A possible theme of the story is that people can overcome obstacles as they journey through life. In the beginning, Mary Lennox is "tyrannical" and "selfish." However, her character begins to change as she "cried and slept" while she witnessed "mysterious and frightening sounds." Change is imminent.

1—A possible theme is that young children can be resilient and can overcome challenges.

0—Children are neglected every day.

28. **Correct Answers: (A)** In the introductory paragraph, Carroll refers to symbolic logic as "a most interesting mental recreation." **(C)** Carroll encourages the reader to work hard in understanding symbolic logic. **(E)** Carroll emphasizes that there are challenges in this type of reading.

29. **Correct Answers: (B)** Carroll uses numerals to organize specific reading strategies that may be used to read symbolic logic. **(F)** Carroll offers suggestions in reading symbolic logic. **(G)** Carroll provides an anecdote to emphasize his point.

30. **Correct Answers: (A)** Carroll explains how reading the story at the end may work for regular reading, but it will not work for symbolic logic. **(C)** Carroll urges the reader to start at the beginning and avoid looking ahead to the end or to any other parts of the story due to the nature of symbolic logic.

31. **Correct Answers: (A)** Carroll is comparing the second reading strategy to a conquered land where the reader understands the message of the story. **(E)** Carroll is using the idea of a conquered land to symbolize mastery.

32. **Correct Answers: (A)** The central idea is that readers must reread the story whenever there is an obstacle in understanding the story. **(B)** The central idea is that brains get tired and need to rest in order to read symbolic logic effectively. **(C)** The central idea is that a mind must be fresh and alert in order to reread and to understand troubling parts of the story. **(D)** The central idea is to reread any parts of the story that are hard to understand.

33. **Correct Answers: (A)** Carroll argues that it is an enjoyable type of reading. **(B)** Carroll argues that even children can enjoy this type of writing and that this reading can challenge the mind and bring clarity of thought. **(D)** Carroll argues that this is an art that should not go unnoticed by potential readers.

34. **Answers will vary.** Below is a sample with a 2, 1, or 0 constructed-response.

    2—The central idea of this passage is that symbolic logic reading is "a most interesting mental recreation" which can be strengthened by following four key reading strategies. This will bring "healthy enjoyment" and "clearness of thought."

    1—The central idea is that symbolic logic can be overcome by using specific reading strategies.

    0—Symbolic logic is helpful.

35. **Answers will vary.** Below is a sample with a 2, 1, or 0 constructed-response.

    2—Symbolic logic reading can be challenging; however, it offers clarity of "thought" in many cases. There are specific reading strategies that may help with this type of writing. One should read from the beginning. Another tip is not to proceed until everything is understood. Reread things that you do not understand. Finally, discuss the story with friends to build on meaning.

    1—Symbolic reading can help improve the mind like a puzzle. There are many reading strategies that one can follow. Children can read symbolic logic writing, too. It is enjoyable.

    0—Symbolic reading is fun.

36. **Answers will vary.** Below is a sample with a 2, 1, or 0 constructed-response.

    2—Carroll's purpose in writing this Introduction is to encourage readers who may be interested in reading symbolic logic. He does this by giving readers four reading strategies such as beginning "at the beginning," proceeding after you "thoroughly understand the whole book," rereading, and discussing the story with a friend. Carroll says that "you may get much healthy enjoyment" from reading symbolic logic.

    1—Carroll's purpose for this Introduction is to express how enjoyable reading symbolic logic is along with offering reading strategies that may help people who are interested in this type of reading.

    0—Mental relaxation is part of symbolic logic.

Performance Task—Part One: pages 136–143

1. **Answers will vary.** Below is a sample with a 2, 1, or 0 constructed-response.

   2—Poe proclaims that his main purpose is to share minor poems that left a "most definite impression" on him. He states that poetry can elevate the "soul" and "excitement" which leaves passion for the reader. Furthermore, Poe explains how long epics are a "nullity" and not ideal. Short poetry, in Poe's eyes, is the most effective type of verse.

   1—Poe argues that short poetry is far better than a longer poem such as an epic. He states that epics do not have the capacity to leave an impression on the reader the way a shorter poem can.

   0—Poetry is beautiful.

2. **Answers will vary.** Below is a sample with a 2, 1, or 0 constructed-response.

   2—Poetry's key impressions on Poe are simple as it is capable of "elevating the soul" and of "elevating excitement." He believes that short poetry can result in "a constant alternation of excitement and depression." Perry believes that poetry can make an "impression, transforming imagination, and expression."

   1—Perry believes that there are "some of the strange potencies of verse: its power."

   0—They believe poetry is nice.

3. **Answers will vary.** Below is a sample with a 2, 1, or 0 constructed-response.

   2—Perry states that "poetry seems to have occupied the attention of me." Poe describes how poetry can leave make an "impression" as well. Differences include Poe's emphasis on the "minor poems," whereas Perry does not make that distinction.

   1—Perry mentions how poetry can "be utilized in the classroom." Poe does not mention education in his essay at all.

   0—Perry and Poe have similarities about poetry.

Performance Task—Part Two: pages 144–145

Poetry Narrative

Answers will vary. Below are samples with a 4, 3, 2, or 1 rubric response.

Rubric Score 4

Lana pulled out a book of American poetry from underneath her back. She had been reading the book when she fell asleep in the woods behind her father's red brick house. She remembered the discussion the class had in her high school English class about Poe's essay on minor poetry. She was a fan of the minor poem as well and read much of Dickinson's poetry over the years. She decided to take a walk through the green trees and bushes that lie quietly within the silent environs. Only the sound of rustling debris resonated in the slow breeze. She was at home in the woods and spent a lot of time reading and writing there.

Beginning a gradual stroll through the woods, Lana lost herself into deep contemplation. She remembered how her class read about Perry's view of poetry likening it to an "impression, transforming imagination, and expression." She could not agree any more than she did. She wondered about the impressions that these great writers felt when reading poetry and continued moving gradually through the woods.

Looking at her feet or part of the walk, Lana turned her head around to stare at a soft patch of tulips planted into the ground. That was definitely odd. What were they doing there? She reached down to touch the tulip, and an airy voice sang out a Dickinson poem! Lana was shocked and a little spooked, so she continued on her walk. Twenty minutes later, she spotted another patch of tulips. Again, she touched the petals, and a Wordsworth poem sang from the tulips. Lana was overwhelmed by the powerful emotions that emanated from the tulips. Lana found three more patches on her way back home.

Being alone was nothing unusual for Lana. She couldn't wait to share her experiences in the woods with her best friend, Lottie. She doubted anyone would believe her, but she had to tell her friend. The phone call was unsuccessful. Lottie did not believe her, and Lana wasn't able to tell her father. Her secret in the woods would have to remain like that, and she sighed as she thought about her solitude and her lonely life filled with lyrical poetry. She drifted off into a peaceful sleep.

Rubric Score 3

Peter rested his head on the marble kitchen counter as his mother lectured him about the day. "Peter, you need to make sure that you get all of your homework done before we leave because there will not be time to do it in the mountains." Peter answered with a bored croak, "Yes, mom." Peter retreated to his room to complete his poetry assignment for English. Peter had to write about the impressions that poetry can make on a person. How was he going to respond to that?

Peter turned on his computer, and began reading the assignment again. He had to write an essay about Poe and Perry's views on poetry in their essays. They were clearly biased, and Peter did not share their enthusiasm for poetry. Perry believed that it transformed "imagination" Poe believed it elevated "excitement." Peter sighed and started writing his essay. His mom had purchased some poetry books for the English unit, so he started reading some of the poetry.

One hour later, Peter finally woke up from a trance. His mother had actually bought a poetry book on horses which was a hobby of his that was close to his heart. The beautiful poetry had actually spoken to him. Closing the poetry book, Peter started typing his essay. With a clear head, he realized that this was probably the best essay he had ever written. His mom knew him well!

Rubric Score 2

There was a boy who loved poetry very much. His nam was Theodire. He was a good student. He worked hard to write good poetry. Sometimes he could write real well. Sometimes he could not. He liked to write. He liked scool. That is where he learned of poetry.

He walked to scooll that day because he had a report. It was fun for him to tallk about poetry. His teecher helped him a lot. He spent most of his day in scool. He liked it.

His report was good. His classmates sed he did it well. He was happy. He did good becuz he had a love of poetry. His excitement helped him a lot. He got a good grade. He was so glad.

Rubric Score 1

Reye likd poems. Rey red it a lot. Reye sed that it was her favorate thing to do. She loved reeding it. She sed she wood rite it one day. She thinks that she can if she reeds a lot of it. It mad her happy. Reye will alwaes try in scool. She was going to work reely hard and then mak a good grad to make her dad prowd.

English Language Arts Standards, Grade 7

Reading: Literature

Key Ideas and Details

CCSS.ELA-LITERACY.RL.7.1 Cite several pieces of textual evidence to support analysis of what the text says explicitly as well as inferences drawn from it.

CCSS.ELA-LITERACY.RL.7.2 Determine a theme or central idea of a text and analyze its development over the course of the text; provide an objective summary of the text.

CCSS.ELA-LITERACY.RL.7.3 Analyze how particular elements of a story or drama interact (e.g., *how setting shapes the characters or plot*).

Craft and Structure

CCSS.ELA-LITERACY.RL.7.4 Determine the meaning of words and phrases as they are used in a text, including figurative and connotative meanings; analyze the impact of rhymes and other repetitions of sounds.

CCSS.ELA-LITERACY.RL.7.5 Analyze how a drama's or poem's form or structure contributes to its meaning.

CCSS.ELA-LITERACY.RL.7.6 Analyze how an author develops and contrasts the points of view of different characters or narrators in a text.

Integration of Knowledge and Ideas

CCSS.ELA-LITERACY.RL.7.7 Compare and contrast a written story, drama, or poem to its audio, filmed, staged, or multimedia version, analyzing effects of techniques unique to each medium.

CCSS.ELA-LITERACY.RL.7.8 (*RL.7.8 not applicable to literature*)

CCSS.ELA-LITERACY.RL.7.9 Compare and contrast a fictional portrayal of a time, place, or character and a historical account of the same period as a means of understanding how authors of fiction use or alter history.

Range of Reading and Level of Text Complexity

CCSS.ELA-LITERACY.RL.7.10 By the end of the year, read and comprehend literature, including stories, dramas, and poems in the grades 6–8 complexity band proficiently, with scaffolding as needed at the high end of the range.

Reading: Informational Text

Key Ideas and Details

CCSS.ELA-LITERACY.RI.7.1 Cite several pieces of textual evidence to support analysis of what the text says explicitly as well as inferences drawn from the text.

CCSS.ELA-LITERACY.RI.7.2 Determine two or more central ideas in a text and analyze their development; provide an objective summary of the text.

CCSS.ELA-LITERACY.RI.7.3 Analyze the interactions between individuals, events, and ideas in a text.

Craft and Structure

CCSS.ELA-LITERACY.RI.7.4 Determine the meaning of words and phrases as they are used in a text, including figurative, connotative, and technical meanings; analyze the impact of a specific word choice on meaning and tone.

CCSS.ELA-LITERACY.RI.7.5 Analyze the structure an author uses to organize a text, including how the major sections contribute to the whole and to the development of ideas.

CCSS.ELA-LITERACY.RI.7.6 Determine an author's point of view or purpose in a text and analyze how the author distinguishes his or her position from that of others.

Integration of Knowledge and Ideas

CCSS.ELA-LITERACY.RI.7.7 Compare and contrast a text to an audio, video, or multimedia version of the text.

CCSS.ELA-LITERACY.RI.7.8 Trace and evaluate the argument and specific claims in a text, assessing whether the reasoning is sound and the evidence is relevant and sufficient to support the claims.

CCSS.ELA-LITERACY.RI.7.9 Analyze how two or more authors writing about the same topic shape their presentations of key information by emphasizing different evidence or advancing different interpretations of facts.

Range of Reading and Level of Text Complexity

CCSS.ELA-LITERACY.RI.7.10 By the end of the year read and comprehend literary nonfiction in the grades 6–8 text complexity band proficiently, with scaffolding as needed at the high end of the range.

Writing

Text Types and Purposes

CCSS.ELA-LITERACY.W.7.1 Write arguments to support claims with clear reasons and relevant evidence.

CCSS.ELA-LITERACY.W.7.1.A Introduce claim(s), acknowledge alternate or opposing claims, and organize the reasons and evidence logically.

CCSS.ELA-LITERACY.W.7.1.B Support claim(s) with logical reasoning and relevant evidence, using accurate, credible sources and demonstrating an understanding of topic or text.

CCSS.ELA-LITERACY.W.7.1.C Use words, phrases, and clauses to create cohesion and clarify the relationships among claim(s), reasons, and evidence.

CCSS.ELA-LITERACY.W.7.1.D Establish and maintain a formal style.

CCSS.ELA-LITERACY.W.7.1.E Provide a concluding statement or section that follows from and supports the argument presented.

CCSS.ELA-LITERACY.W.7.2 Write informative/explanatory texts to examine a topic and convey ideas, concepts, and information through the selection, organization, and analysis of relevant content.

CCSS.ELA-LITERACY.W.7.2.A Introduce a topic clearly, previewing what is to follow; organize ideas, concepts, and information, using strategies such as definition, classification, comparison/contrast, and cause/effect. Include formatting and multimedia when useful to aiding comprehension.

CCSS.ELA-LITERACY.W.7.2.B Develop the topic with relevant facts, definitions, concrete details, quotations, or other information and examples.

CCSS.ELA-LITERACY.W.7.2.C Use appropriate transitions to create cohesion and clarify the relationships among ideas and concepts.

CCSS.ELA-LITERACY.W.7.2.D Use precise language and domain-specific vocabulary to inform or explain the topic.

CCSS.ELA-LITERACY.W.7.2.E Establish and maintain a formal style.

CCSS.ELA-LITERACY.W.7.2.F Provide a concluding statement or section that follows from and supports the information or explanation presented.

CCSS.ELA-LITERACY.W.7.3 Write narratives to develop real or imagined experiences or events using effective techniques, relevant descriptive details, and well-structured event sequences.

CCSS.ELA-LITERACY.W.7.3.A Engage the reader by establishing a context and point of view and introducing a narrator and/or characters; organize an event sequence that unfolds naturally.

CCSS.ELA-LITERACY.W.7.3.B Use narrative techniques, such as dialogue, pacing, and description to develop experiences, events, or characters.

CCSS.ELA-LITERACY.W.7.3.C Use a variety of transition words, phrases, and clauses to convey sequence and signal shifts from one time frame or setting to another.

CCSS.ELA-LITERACY.W.7.3.D Use precise words and phrases, relevant descriptive details, and sensory language to capture the action and convey experiences and events.

CCSS.ELA-LITERACY.W.7.3.E Provide a conclusion that follows from and reflects on the narrated experiences or events.

Production and Distribution of Writing

CCSS.ELA-LITERACY.W.7.4 Produce clear and coherent writing in which the development, organization, and style are appropriate to task, purpose, and audience.

CCSS.ELA-LITERACY.W.7.5 With guidance and support from peers and adults, develop and strengthen writing as needed by panning, revising, editing, rewriting, or trying a new approach. (*Editing for conventions should demonstrate the command of Language standards 1–3 up to and including grade 7.*)

CCSS.ELA-LITERACY.W.7.6 Use technology, including the Internet, to produce and publish writing and link to and cite sources as well as interact and collaborate with others.

Research to Build and Present Knowledge

CCSS.ELA-LITERACY.W.7.7 Conduct short research projects to answer a question using several sources and generate additional questions for further research and investigation.

CCSS.ELA-LITERACY.W.7.8 Gather relevant information from multiple print and digital sources and quote or paraphrase the data and conclusions of others by avoiding plagiarism and following a format for citation.

CCSS.ELA-LITERACY.W.7.9 Draw evidence from literary or informational texts to support analysis, reflection, and research.

CCSS.ELA-LITERACY.W.7.9.A Apply grade 7 Reading standards to literature (e.g., "*Compare and contrast a fictional time, place, or character and a historical account of the same period as a means of understanding how authors of fiction use or alter history*").

CCSS.ELA-LITERACY.W.7.9.B Apply grade 7 Reading standards to literary nonfiction (e.g., "*Trace and evaluate the argument and specific claims in a text, assessing whether the reasoning is sound and the evidence is relevant and sufficient to support the claims*").

Range of Writing

CCSS.ELA-LITERACY.W.7.10 Write routinely over extended time frames (*time for research, reflection, and revision*) and shorter time frames (*a single sitting or a day or two*) for a range of discipline-specific tasks, purposes, and audiences.

Speaking and Listening

Comprehension and Collaboration

CCSS.ELA-LITERACY.SL.7.1 Engage effectively in a range of collaborative discussions (*one-on-one, in groups, and teacher-led*) with diverse partners on grade 7 topics, texts, and issues, building on others' ideas and expressing their own clearly.

CCSS.ELA-LITERACY.SL.7.1.A Come to discussions prepared, having read or researched material; explicitly draw on that preparation by referring to evidence on the topic, text, or issue to prove and reflect on ideas under discussion.

CCSS.ELA-LITERACY.SL.7.1.B Follow rules for collegial discussions, track progress toward specific goals and deadlines, and define individual roles as needed.

CCSS.ELA-LITERACY.SL.7.1.C Pose questions that elicit elaboration and respond to others' questions with relevant observations and ideas that bring the discussion back on topic as needed.

CCSS.ELA-LITERACY.SL.7.1.D Acknowledge new information expressed by others and, when warranted, modify their own views.

CCSS.ELA-LITERACY.SL.7.2 Analyze the main ideas and supporting details presented in diverse media and formats and explain how the ideas clarify a topic, text, or issue under study.

CCSS.ELA-LITERACY.SL.7.3 Delineate a speaker's argument and specific claims, evaluating the soundness of the reasoning and the relevance and sufficiency of the evidence.

Presentation of Knowledge and Ideas

CCSS.ELA-LITERACY.SL.7.4 Present claims and findings, emphasizing salient points in a focused, coherent manner with pertinent descriptions, facts, details, and examples; use appropriate eye contact, adequate volume, and clear pronunciation.

CCSS.ELA-LITERACY.SL.7.5 Include multimedia components and visual displays in presentations to clarify claims and findings and emphasize salient points.

CCSS.ELA-LITERACY.SL.7.6 Adapt speech to a variety of contexts and tasks, demonstrating command of formal English when indicated or appropriate. (*See grade 7 Language standards 1 and 3 for specific expectations.*)

Language

Conventions of Standard English

CCSS.ELA-LITERACY.L.7.1 Demonstrate command of the conventions of Standard English grammar and usage when writing or speaking.

CCSS.ELA-LITERACY.L.7.1.A Explain the function of phrases and clauses in general and their function in specific sentences.

CCSS.ELA-LITERACY.L.7.1.B Choose among simple, compound, complex, and compound-complex sentences to signal differing relationships among ideas.

CCSS.ELA-LITERACY.L.7.1.C Place phrases and clauses within a sentence, recognizing and correcting misplaced and dangling modifiers.

CCSS.ELA-LITERACY.L.7.2 Demonstrate command of the conventions of Standard English capitalization, punctuation, and spelling when writing.

CCSS.ELA-LITERACY.L.7.2.A Use a comma to separate coordinate adjectives (e.g., *It was a fascinating, enjoyable movie but he wore an old[,] green shirt*).

CCSS.ELA-LITERACY.L.7.2.B Spell correctly.

CCSS.ELA-LITERACY.L.7.3 Use knowledge of language and its conventions when writing, speaking, reading, or listening.

CCSS.ELA-LITERACY.L.7.3.A Choose language that expresses ideas precisely and concisely, recognizing and eliminating wordiness and redundancy.

Vocabulary Acquisition and Use

CCSS.ELA-LITERACY.L.7.4 Determine or clarify the meaning of unknown multiple-meaning words and phrases based on grade 7 reading and content, choosing flexibly from a range of strategies.

CCSS.ELA-LITERACY.L.7.4.A Use context (e.g., *the overall meaning of a sentence or paragraph; a word's position or function in a sentence*) as a clue to the meaning of a word or phrase.

CCSS.ELA-LITERACY.L.7.4.B Use common, grade-appropriate Greek or Latin affixes and roots as clues to the meaning of a word.

CCSS.ELA-LITERACY.L.7.4.C Consult reference materials (e.g., *dictionaries, glossaries, thesauruses*), both print and digital, to find the pronunciation of a word or determine its precise meaning or part of speech.

CCSS.ELA-LITERACY.L.7.4.D Verify the preliminary determination of the meaning of a word or phrase (e.g., *by checking the inferred meaning in context or in a dictionary*).

CCSS.ELA-LITERACY.L.7.5 Demonstrate understanding of figurative language, word relationships, and nuances in word meanings.

CCSS.ELA-LITERACY.L.7.5.A Interpret figures of speech (e.g., *literary, biblical, and mythological allusions*) in context.

CCSS.ELA-LITERACY.L.7.5.B Use the relationship between particular words (e.g., *synonym/antonym, analogy*) to better understand each of the words.

CCSS.ELA-LITERACY.L.7.5.C Distinguish among the connotations (associations) of words with similar denotations (*definitions*) (e.g., *refined, respectful, polite, diplomatic, condescending*).

CCSS.ELA-LITERACY.L.7.6 Acquire and use accurately grade-appropriate general academic and domain-specific words and phrases; gather vocabulary knowledge when considering a word or phrase important to comprehension and expression.

Smarter Balanced Scoring Rubrics

Smarter Balanced Scoring Rubrics (Grades 6-11)

	4-Point Argumentative Writing Rubric
Score	Purpose/Organization
4	The response is fully sustained and consistently and purposefully focused. The response has a clear and effective organizational structure creating unity and completeness. > claim is clearly stated, focused, and strongly maintained > alternate or opposing claims are clearly addressed > claim is introduced and communicated clearly within the context > effective, consistent use of a variety of transitional strategies > logical progression of ideas from beginning to end > effective introduction and conclusion for audience and purpose > strong connections among ideas, with some syntactic variety
3	The response is adequately sustained and generally focused. The response has an evident organizational structure and a sense of completeness, though there may be minor flaws and some ideas may be loosely connected. > claim is clear and for the most part maintained, though some loosely related material may be present > context provided for the claim is adequate > adequate use of transitional strategies with some variety > adequate progression of ideas from beginning to end > adequate introduction and conclusion > adequate, if slightly inconsistent, connection among ideas

2	The response is somewhat sustained and may have a minor drift in focus. The response has an inconsistent organizational structure, and flaws are evident.
	> may be clearly focused on the claim but is insufficiently sustained
	> claim on the issue may be somewhat unclear and unfocused
	> inconsistent use of basic transitional strategies with little variety
	> uneven progression of ideas from beginning to end
	> conclusion and introduction, if present, are weak
	> weak connection among ideas
1	The response may be related to the purpose but may offer little relevant detail. The response has little or no discernible organizational structure.
	> may be very brief
	> may have a major drift
	> claim may be confusing or ambiguous
	> few or no transitional strategies are evident
	> frequent extraneous ideas may intrude
NS	A response gets no credit if it provides no evidence of the ability to be focused and organized.
Score	Language and Elaboration
4	The response provides thorough and convincing support/evidence for the writer's claim that includes effective use of sources, facts, and details. The response achieves substantial depth that is specific and relevant. The response clearly and effectively expresses ideas, using precise language.
	> use of evidence from sources is smoothly integrated, comprehensive, relevant, and concrete
	> effective use of a variety of elaborative techniques
	> use of academic and domain-specific vocabulary is clearly appropriate for the audience and purpose

3	The response provides adequate support/evidence for the writer's claim that includes the use of sources, facts, and details. The response achieves some depth and specificity but is predominately general. The response adequately expresses ideas, employing a mix of precise with more general language. > some evidence from sources is integrated, though citations may be general or imprecise > adequate use of some elaborative techniques > use of domain-specific vocabulary is generally appropriate for the audience and purpose
2	The response provides uneven, cursory support/evidence for the writer's claim that includes partial or uneven use of sources, facts, and details, and achieves little depth. The response expresses ideas unevenly, using simplistic language. > evidence from sources is weakly integrated, and citations, if present, are uneven > weak or uneven use of elaborative techniques > use of domain-specific vocabulary may at times be inappropriate for the audience and purpose
1	The response provides minimal support/evidence for the writer's claim that includes little or no use of sources, facts, and details. The response expression of ideas is vague, lacks clarity, or is confusing. > use of evidence from sources is minimal, absent, in error, or irrelevant > uses limited language or domain-specific vocabulary > may have little sense of audience and purpose
NS	A response gets no credit if it provides no evidence of the ability to respond with support/evidence to the writer's claim and include expression of idea and language.

Score	Conventions
4	**The response demonstrates a strong command of conventions.** > few, if any, errors are present in usage and sentence formation > effective and consistent use of punctuation, capitalization, and spelling
3	**The response demonstrates an adequate command of conventions.** > some errors in usage and sentence formation may be present, but no systematic pattern of errors is displayed > adequate use of punctuation, capitalization, and spelling
2	**The response demonstrates a partial command of conventions.** > frequent errors in usage, may obscure meaning > inconsistent use of punctuation, capitalization, and spelling
1	**The response demonstrates a lack of command and conventions.** > errors are frequent and severe and meaning is often obscure
NS	**A response gets no credit if it provides no evidence of proper use of language conventions.**

4-Point Informative Explanatory Writing Rubric	
Score	**Purpose/Organization**
4	**The response is fully sustained and consistently and purposefully focused. The response has a clear and effective organizational structure creating unity and completeness.** > controlling idea or main idea of a topic is focused, clearly stated, and strongly maintained > controlling idea or main idea of a topic is introduced and communicated clearly within the context > use of a variety of transitional strategies > logical progression of ideas from beginning to end > effective introduction and conclusion for audience and purpose > strong connections among ideas, with some syntactic variety

3	The response is adequately sustained and generally focused. The response has an evident organizational structure and a sense of completeness, though there may be minor flaws and some ideas may be loosely connected.
	> focus is clear and for the most part maintained, though some loosely related material may be present
	> some context for the controlling idea or main idea of the topic is adequate
	> adequate use of transitional strategies with some variety
	> adequate progression of ideas from beginning to end
	> adequate introduction and conclusion
	> adequate, if slightly inconsistent, connection among ideas
2	The response is somewhat sustained and may have a minor drift in focus. The response has an inconsistent organizational structure, and flaws are evident.
	> may be clearly focused on the controlling or main idea, but is insufficiently sustained
	> controlling idea or main idea may be unclear and somewhat unfocused
	> inconsistent use of transitional strategies with little variety
	> uneven progression of ideas from beginning to end
	> conclusion and introduction, if present, are weak
	> weak connection among ideas
1	The response may be related to the topic but may provide little or no focus. The response has little or no discernible organizational structure.
	> may be very brief
	> may have a major drift
	> focus may be confusing or ambiguous
	> few or no transitional strategies are evident
	> frequent extraneous ideas may intrude
NS	A response gets no credit if it provides no evidence of the ability to provide a response that is sustained, focused, and organized.

Score	Language and Elaboration
4	The response provides thorough and convincing support/evidence for the controlling idea or main idea that includes the effective use of sources, facts, and details. The response achieves substantial depth that is specific and relevant. The response clearly and effectively expresses ideas, using precise language. › use of evidence from sources is smoothly integrated, comprehensive, and concrete › effective use of a variety of elaborative techniques › use of academic and domain-specific vocabulary is clearly appropriate for the audience and purpose
3	The response provides adequate support/evidence for the controlling idea or main idea that includes use of sources, facts, and details. The response adequately expresses ideas, employing a mix of precise with more general language. › some evidence from sources is integrated, though citations may be general and imprecise › adequate use of some elaborative techniques › use of domain-specific vocabulary is generally appropriate for the audience and purpose
2	The response provides uneven, cursory support/evidence for the controlling or main idea that includes partial or uneven use of sources, facts, and details. The response expresses ideas unevenly, using simplistic language. › evidence from sources is weakly integrated, and citations, if present, are uneven › weak or uneven use of elaborative techniques › use of domain-specific vocabulary that may at times be inappropriate for the audience and purpose
1	The response provides minimal support/evidence for the controlling or main idea that includes little or no use of sources, facts, and details. The response expression of ideas is vague, lacks clarity, or is confusing. › use of evidence from the source material is minimal, absent, in error, or irrelevant › uses limited language or domain-specific vocabulary › may have little sense of audience and purpose

NS	A response gets no credit if it provides no evidence or the ability to provide support/evidence for the controlling or main idea and use academic or domain-specific vocabulary.
Score	**Conventions**
4	**The response demonstrates a strong command of conventions.** > few, if any, errors are present in usage and sentence formation > effective and consistent use of punctuation, capitalization, and spelling
3	**The response demonstrates an adequate command of conventions.** > some errors in usage and sentence formation may be present, but no systematic pattern of errors is displayed > adequate use of punctuation, capitalization, and spelling
2	**The response demonstrates a partial command of conventions.** > frequent errors in usage may obscure meaning > inconsistent use of punctuation, capitalization, and spelling
1	**The response demonstrates a lack of command of conventions.** > errors are frequent and severe and meaning is often obscure
NS	A response gets no credit if it provides no evidence of the ability to demonstrate strong command of conventions and effective, consistent use of punctuation, capitalization, and spelling.

4-Point Narrative Writing Rubric	
Score	**Focus/Organization**
4	**The narrative, real or imagined, is clearly focused and maintained throughout. The narrative, real or imagined, has an effective plot helping create unity and completeness.** > effectively establishes a setting, narrator and/or characters, and point of view > effective, consistent use of a variety of transitional strategies > logical sequence of events from beginning to end > effective opening and closure for audience and purpose

3	The narrative, real or imagined, is adequately focused and generally maintained throughout. The narrative, real or imagined, has an evident plot helping create a sense of unity and completeness, though there may be minor flaws and some ideas may be loosely connected. > adequately establishes a setting, narrator and/or characters, and point of view > adequate use of a variety of transitional strategies > adequate sequence of events from beginning to end > adequate opening and closure for audience and purpose
2	The narrative, real or imagined, is somewhat maintained and may have a minor drift in focus. The narrative, real or imagined, has an inconsistent plot, and flaws are evident. > inconsistently establishes a setting, narrator and/or characters, and point of view > inconsistent use of basic transitional strategies with little variety > uneven sequence of events from beginning to end > opening and closure, if present, are weak > weak connection among ideas
1	The narrative, real or imagined, may be maintained but may provide little or no focus. The narrative, real or imagined, has little or no discernible plot. > may be very brief > may have a major drift > focus may be confusing or ambiguous > few or no transitional strategies are evident > frequent extraneous ideas may intrude
NS	A response gets no credit if it provides no evidence of the ability to provide a narrative, real or imagined, with focus throughout and an effective plot.

Score	Elaboration and Language
4	The narrative, real or imagined, provides thorough and effective elaboration using details, dialogue, and description. The narrative, real or imagined, clearly and effectively expresses experiences or events. > effective use of a variety of narrative techniques that advance the story or illustrate the experience > effective use of sensory, concrete, and figurative language that clearly advances the purpose
3	The narrative, real or imagined, provides adequate elaboration using details, dialogue, and description. The narrative, real or imagined, adequately expresses experiences or events. > adequate use of a variety of narrative techniques that generally advance the story or illustrate the experience > adequate use of sensory, concrete, and figurative language that generally advances the purpose
2	The narrative, real or imagined, provides uneven, cursory elaboration using partial and uneven details, dialogue, and description. The narrative, real or imagined, unevenly expresses experiences or events. > narrative techniques, if present, are uneven and inconsistent > partial or weak use of sensory, concrete, and figurative language that may not advance the purpose
1	The narrative, real or imagined, provides minimal elaboration using little or no details, dialogue, and description. The narrative, real or imagined, expression of ideas is vague, lacks clarity, or is confusing. > use of narrative techniques is minimal, absent, in error, or irrelevant > uses limited language > may have little sense of purpose
NS	A response gets no credit if it provides no evidence of the ability to effectively establish a setting, narrator and/or characters, and point of view, and does not contain a plot that helps create unity and completeness.

Score	Conventions
4	The narrative, real or imagined, demonstrates a strong command of conventions. > few, if any, errors in usage and sentence formation > effective and consistent use of punctuation, capitalization, and spelling
3	The narrative, real or imagined, demonstrates an adequate command of conventions. > some errors in usage and sentence formation but no systematic pattern of errors is displayed > adequate use of punctuation, capitalization, and spelling
2	The narrative, real or imagined, demonstrates a partial command of conventions. > frequent errors in usage may obscure meaning > inconsistent use of punctuation, capitalization, and spelling
1	The narrative, real or imagined, demonstrates a lack of command of conventions. > errors are frequent and severe and meaning is often obscured
NS	A response gets no credit if it provides no evidence of the ability to demonstrate a command of conventions: use of punctuation, capitalization, and spelling.

Performance Task Writing Rubrics

How to Use the Smarter Balanced Performance Task Writing Rubrics

When the SBAC scores your writing, there are certain skills and elements that they look for. A rubric organizes these elements by level of mastery. Each level of mastery is given a score. It is helpful for you to understand these different levels so you can write with these expectations in mind. Actually, it is encouraged to treat the rubrics as a checklist. When you are done with your writing, check it against each element in the rubric.

There are three different rubrics: Informative Writing, Opinion Writing, and Narrative Writing. The Informative and Opinion rubrics are divided into three areas (Purpose/Organization, Evidence/Elaboration, and Conventions). The Purpose/Organization and Evidence/Elaboration sections range in scores from 1 to 4, with 4 being the highest. The Conventions section ranges from 0 to 2, with 2 being the highest. When you read each section to assess your own writing, pay attention to the progression of adjectives to describe each element of writing. For instance, in the Purpose/Organization section, the element of transitional strategies (i.e., *then*, *furthermore*, *in conclusion*, etc.) progresses from a 1 score with "no" strategies used to a 2 score with an "inconsistent use" of strategies to a 3 score with an "adequate use" of strategies to a 4 score with a "consistent use" of strategies. This pattern is the same for each writing element in the rubrics. Knowing these for each element will help you assess, or score, your own writing.

Each of these areas can have their own score. For example, a student could receive a 4 for Purpose/Organization, but only receive a 2 for Evidence/Elaboration. Let's say the student also receives a score of 1 for Conventions. The total for all three areas is 10. This student, then, scored a 7 out of 10.

Let's look at the specific areas to get a better understanding of SBAC writing expectations.

Smarter Balanced Performance Task Rubric (Grades 6–11)

	4-Point Argumentative Performance Task Rubric
Score	**Purpose/Organization**
4	The response has a clear and effective organizational structure, creating a sense of unity and completeness. The organization is fully sustained and consistently and purposefully focused. > claim is introduced, clearly communicated, and the focus is strongly maintained for the purpose and audience > consistent use of a variety of transitional strategies to clarify the relationships between and among ideas > effective introduction and conclusion > logical progression of ideas from beginning to end; strong connections between and among ideas with some syntactic variety > alternate and opposing argument(s) clearly acknowledged or addressed
3	The response has an evident organizational structure and a sense of completeness. Though there may be minor flaws, they do not interfere with the overall coherence. The response is generally focused. > claim is clear, and the focus is mostly maintained for the purpose and audience > adequate use of transitional strategies with some variety to clarify relationships between and among ideas > adequate introduction and conclusion > adequate progression of ideas from beginning to end; adequate connections between and among ideas > alternate and opposing argument(s) are adequately acknowledged or addressed

2	The response has an inconsistent organizational structure. Some flaws are evident and some ideas may be loosely connected. The organization is somewhat sustained between paragraphs and may have a minor drift in focus.
	> claim may be somewhat unclear or the focus may be insufficiently sustained for the purpose and/or audience
	> inconsistent use of transitional strategies
	> introduction or conclusion may be weak
	> uneven progression of ideas from beginning to end
	> alternate and opposing argument(s) may be confusing or not acknowledged
1	The response has little or no discernible organizational structure. The response may be related to the claim, but may provide little or no focus.
	> claim may be confusing, ambiguous, or brief or the focus may drift from the purpose and/or audience
	> few or no transitional strategies are evident
	> introduction and/or conclusion may be missing
	> frequent extraneous ideas may be evident; ideas may be randomly ordered or have unclear progression
	> alternate and opposing argument(s) may not be acknowledged
NS	> Insufficient
	> In a language other than English
	> Off-topic
	> Off-purpose
Score	**Evidence/Elaboration**
4	The response provides thorough and convincing elaboration of the evidence for the claim and argument(s), including reasoned, in-depth analysis and the effective use of source material. The response clearly and effectively develops ideas using precise language.
	> comprehensive evidence from the source material is integrated, relevant, and specific
	> clear citations or attribution to source material
	> effective use of a variety of elaborative techniques
	> vocabulary is clearly appropriate for the audience and purpose
	> effective and appropriate style enhances content

3	The response provides adequate elaboration of the evidence for the claim and argument(s) that include reasoned analysis and the use of source material. The response adequately develops ideas, employing a mix of precise, more general language. > adequate evidence (facts and details) from the source material is integrated and irrelevant, yet may be general > adequate use of citations > adequate use of some elaborative techniques > vocabulary is generally appropriate for the audience and purpose > generally appropriate style is evident
2	The response provides uneven, cursory elaboration of the support/evidence for the claim and argument(s) that include some reasoned analysis and partial or uneven use of source material. The response develops ideas unevenly, using simplistic language. > some evidence (facts and details) from the source material may be weakly integrated, imprecise, repetitive, vague, and/or copied > weak use of citations or attribution to source material > weak or uneven use of elaborative techniques; development may consist primarily of source summary or may rely on emotional appeal > vocabulary use is uneven or somewhat ineffective for the audience and purpose > inconsistent or weak attempt to create appropriate style
1	The response provides minimal elaboration of the support/evidence for the claim and argument(s) that include little or no use of source material. The response is vague, lacks clarity, or is confusing. > evidence (facts and details) from the source material is minimal, irrelevant, absent, incorrectly used, or predominately copied > insufficient use of citations or attribution to source material > minimal use of elaborative techniques; emotional appeal may dominate > vocabulary is limited or ineffective for the audience or purpose > little or no evidence of appropriate style
NS	> Insufficient (includes copied) text > In a language other than English > Off-topic > Off-purpose

Acknowledging and/or addressing the opposing point of view begins at grade 7.

Score	2-Point Argumentative Performance Task Writing Rubric (Grades 6-11)
	Conventions
2	**The response demonstrates an adequate command of conventions.** > adequate use of correct sentence formation, punctuation, capitalization, grammar usage, and spelling
1	**The response demonstrates a partial command of conventions.** > limited use of correct sentence formation, punctuation, capitalization, grammar usage, and spelling
0	**The response demonstrates little or no command of conventions.** > infrequent use of correct sentence formation, punctuation, capitalization, grammar usage, and spelling
NS	> Insufficient (includes copied) text > In a language other than English > Off-topic > Off-purpose

Holistic Scoring:

> **Variety:** A range of errors includes sentence formation, punctuation, capitalization, grammar usage, and spelling.
> **Severity:** Basic errors are more heavily weighted than higher-level errors.
> **Density:** The proportion of errors to the amount of writing done well. This includes the ratio of errors to the length of the piece.

	4-Point Explanatory Performance Task Writing Rubric (Grades 6–11)
Score	**Purpose/Organization**
4	**The response has a clear and effective organizational structure, creating a sense of unity and completeness. The organization is fully sustained between and within paragraphs. The response is consistently and purposefully focused.** > thesis/controlling idea of a topic is clearly communicated, and the focus is strongly maintained for the purpose and audience > consistent use of a variety of transitional strategies to clarify the relationships between and among ideas > effective introduction and conclusion > logical progression of ideas from beginning to end; strong connections between and among ideas with some syntactic variety
3	**The response has an evident organizational structure and a sense of completeness. Though there may be minor flaws, they do not interfere with the overall coherence. The organization is adequately sustained between and within paragraphs. The response is generally focused.** > thesis/controlling idea of a topic is clear, and the focus is mostly maintained for the purpose and audience > adequate use of transitional strategies with some variety to clarify the relationships between and among ideas > adequate introduction and conclusion > adequate progression of ideas from beginning to end and adequate connections among ideas
2	**The response has an inconsistent organizational structure. Some flaws are evident, and some ideas may be loosely connected. The organization is somewhat sustained between and within paragraphs. The response may have a minor drift in focus.** > thesis/controlling idea of a topic may be somewhat unclear, or the focus may be insufficiently sustained for the purpose or audience > inconsistent use of transitional strategies and/or little variety > introduction or conclusion, if present, may be weak > uneven progression of ideas from beginning to end and/or formulaic; inconsistent or unclear connections between and among ideas

1	The response has little or no discernible organizational structure. The response may be related to the topic but may provide little or no focus.
	> thesis/controlling idea may be confusing or ambiguous; response may be too brief or the focus may drift from the purpose and/or audience
	> few or no transitional strategies are evident
	> introduction and/or conclusion may be missing
	> frequent extraneous ideas may be evident; ideas may be randomly ordered or have an unclear progression
NS	> Insufficient (includes copied text)
	> In a language other than English
	> Off-topic
	> Off-purpose
Score	**Evidence/Elaboration**
4	The response provides thorough elaboration of the support/evidence for the thesis/controlling idea that includes the effective use of source material. The response clearly and effectively develops ideas using precise language.
	> comprehensive evidence (facts and details) from the source material is integrated, relevant, and specific
	> clear citations or attribution to source material
	> vocabulary is clearly appropriate for the audience and purpose
	> effective, appropriate style enhances content
3	The response provides adequate elaboration of the support/evidence for the thesis/controlling idea that includes the use of source material. The response adequately develops ideas, employing a mix of precise and more general language.
	> adequate evidence (facts and details) from the source material is integrated and relevant, yet may be general
	> adequate use of citations or attribution to source material
	> adequate use of elaborative techniques
	> vocabulary is generally appropriate for the audience and purpose
	> generally appropriate style is evident

2	The response provides uneven, cursory elaboration of the support/evidence for the thesis/controlling idea that includes uneven or limited source material. The response develops ideas unevenly, using simplistic language.
	> some evidence (facts and details) from the source material may be weakly integrated, imprecise, repetitive, vague, and/or copied
	> weak use of citations or attribution to source material
	> weak or uneven use of elaborative techniques; development may consist primarily of source summary
	> vocabulary use is uneven or somewhat ineffective for the audience or purpose
	> inconsistent or weak attempt to create appropriate style
1	The response provides minimal elaboration of the support/evidence for the thesis/controlling idea that includes little or no use of source material. The response is vague, lacks clarity, or is confusing.
	> evidence (facts and details) from the source material is minimal, irrelevant, absent, incorrectly used, or predominantly copied
	> insufficient use of citations or attribution to source material
	> minimal, if any, use of elaborative techniques
	> vocabulary is limited or ineffective for the audience and purpose
	> little or no evidence of appropriate style
NS	> Insufficient (includes copied text)
	> In a language other than English
	> Off-topic
	> Off-purpose

	2-Point Explanatory Performance Task Writing Rubric (Grades 6–11)
Score	**Conventions**
2	**The response demonstrates an adequate command of conventions.** > adequate use of correct sentence formation, punctuation, capitalization, grammar usage, and spelling
1	**The response demonstrates a partial command of conventions.** > limited use of correct sentence formation, punctuation, capitalization, grammar usage, and spelling
0	**The response demonstrates little or no command of conventions.** > infrequent use of correct sentence formation, punctuation, capitalization, grammar usage, and spelling
NS	> Insufficient (includes copied) text > In a language other than English > Off-topic > Off- purpose

Holistic Scoring:

> **Variety:** A range of errors includes sentence formation, punctuation, capitalization, grammar usage, and spelling.

> **Severity:** Basic errors are more heavily weighted than higher-level errors.

> **Density:** The proportion of errors to the amount of writing done well. This includes the ratio of errors to the length of the piece.

	4-Point Narrative Performance Task Writing Rubric (Grades 3–8)
Score	**Purpose/Organization**
4	**The organization of the narrative, real or imagined, is fully sustained and the focus is clear and maintained throughout:** > an effective plot helps to create a sense of unity and completeness > effectively establishes and maintains setting, develops narrator/characters, and maintains point of view* > consistent use of a variety of transitional strategies to clarify the relationships between and among ideas; strong connection between and among ideas > natural, logical sequence of events from beginning to end > effective opening and closure for audience and purpose
3	**The organization of the narrative, real or imagined, is adequately sustained, and the focus is adequate and generally maintained:** > an evident plot helps to create a sense of unity and completeness, though there may be minor flaws and some ideas may be loosely connected > adequately maintains a setting, develops narrator/characters, and/or maintains point of view* > adequate use of a variety of transitional strategies to clarify the relationships between and among ideas > adequate sequence of events from beginning to end > adequate opening and closure for audience and purpose
2	**The organization of the narrative, real or imagined, is somewhat sustained and may have an uneven focus:** > there may be an inconsistent plot, and/or flaws may be evident > unevenly or minimally maintains a setting, develops narrator and/or characters, and/or maintains point of view* > uneven use of appropriate transitional strategies and/or little variety > weak or uneven sequence of events > opening and closure, if present, are weak

*Point of view begins at grade 7.

1	The organization of the narrative, real or imagined, may be maintained but may provide little or no focus: > there is little or no discernible plot or there may just be a series of events > may be brief or there is little to no attempt to establish a setting, narrator and/or characters, and/or point of view* > few or no appropriate transitional strategies may be evident > little or no organization of an event sequence; frequent extraneous ideas and/or a major drift may be evident > opening and/or closure may be missing
NS	> Unintelligible > In a language other than English > Off-topic > Copied text > Off-purpose
Score	**Development/Elaboration**
4	The narrative, real or imagined, provides thorough, effective elaboration using relevant details, dialogue, and description: > experiences, characters, setting, and events are clearly developed > connections to source materials may enhance the narrative > effective use of a variety of narrative techniques that advance the story or illustrate the experience > effective use of sensory, concrete, and figurative language that clearly advances the purpose > effective, appropriate style enhances the narration
3	The narrative, real or imagined, provides adequate elaboration using details, dialogue, and description: > experiences, characters, setting, and events are adequately developed > connections to source materials may contribute to the narrative > adequate use of a variety of narrative techniques that generally advance the story or illustrate the experience > adequate use of sensory, concrete, and figurative language that generally advances the purpose > generally appropriate style is evident

Elaborative techniques may include the use of personal experiences that support the controlling idea.

*Point of view begins at grade 7.

2	The narrative, real or imagined, provides uneven, cursory elaboration using partial and uneven details, dialogue, and description.	
	> experiences, characters, setting, and events are unevenly developed	
	> connections to source materials may be ineffective, awkward, or vague but do not interfere with the narrative	
	> narrative techniques are uneven and inconsistent	
	> partial or weak use of sensory, concrete, and figurative language that may not advance the purpose	
	> inconsistent or weak attempt to create appropriate style	
1	The narrative, real or imagined, provides minimal elaboration using few or no details, dialogue, and/or description.	
	> experiences, characters, setting, and events may be vague, lack clarity, or confusing	
	> connections to source materials, if evident, may detract from the narrative	
	> use of narrative techniques may be minimal, absent, incorrect, or irrelevant	
	> may have little or no use of sensory, concrete, or figurative language; language does not advance and may interfere with the purpose	
	> little or no evidence of appropriate style	
NS	> Unintelligible	
	> In a language other than English	
	> Off-topic	
	> Copied text	
	> Off-purpose	

Score	2-Point Narrative Performance Task Writing Rubric (Grades 3–11) Conventions
2	**The response demonstrates an adequate command of conventions:** > adequate use of correct sentence formation, punctuation, capitalization, grammar usage, and spelling
1	**The response demonstrates a partial command of conventions:** > limited use of correct sentence formation, punctuation, capitalization, grammar usage, and spelling
0	**The response demonstrates little or no command of conventions:** > infrequent use of correct sentence formation, punctuation, capitalization, grammar usage, and spelling
NS	> Unintelligible > In a language other than English > Off-topic > Copied text (Off-purpose responses will still receive a score in Conventions.)

Holistic Scoring:
> **Variety:** A range of errors includes sentence formation, punctuation, capitalization, grammar usage, and spelling.
> **Severity:** Basic errors are more heavily weighted than higher-level errors.
> **Density:** The proportion of errors to the amount of writing done well. This includes the ratio of errors to the length of the piece.

Overall Claim for Grades 3–8

"Students can demonstrate progress toward college and career readiness in English language arts literacy."

Claim #1—Reading

"Students can read closely and analytically to comprehend a range of increasingly complex literary and informational texts."

Claim #2—Writing

"Students can produce effective and well-grounded writing for a range of purposes and audiences."

Claim #3—Speaking and Listening

"Students can employ effective speaking and listening skills for a range of purposes and audiences."

Claim #4—Research/Inquiry

"Students can engage in research and inquiry to investigate topics, and to analyze, integrate, and present information."

Index

Test Practice for Common Core

GRADE 7 TEST PRACTICE FOR COMMON CORE

Covers Both ELA & Math

Help students practice and prepare for the all-important Common Core assessment tests at the end of the school year. Every turn of the page provides a new standard with a series of practice questions for students to work on. Features include:

- Hundreds of practice questions complete with detailed answers

- Covers many different question types, including multiple-choice, short-answer, extended-response, and more

- Tip boxes throughout the book provide students with friendly reminders

- Easy-to-follow tabs allow parents and teachers to recognize the types of questions within each standard

- An easy-to-follow, side-by-side layout lets students conquer one standard at a time

- Student-friendly worksheets reinforce what they are learning in the classroom

- Practice tests at the end of each section pinpoint strengths and weaknesses

- A cumulative assessment tests their understanding of everything they have learned

Paperback, 8 3/8" x 10 7/8", ISBN 978-1-4380-0706-9
$14.99, *Can$17.99*

It's an excellent resource for parents and teachers as they help students meet and exceed grade level expectations on the Common Core assessment tests.

Available at your local book store or visit www.barronseduc.com

Barron's Educational Series, Inc.
250 Wireless Blvd.
Hauppauge, N.Y. 11788
Order toll-free: 1-800-645-3476

Prices subject to change without notice.

In Canada:
Georgetown Book Warehouse
34 Armstrong Ave.
Georgetown, Ontario L7G 4R9
Canadian orders: 1-800-247-7160

(#309d) R5/16